Sūrah Yā Sīn

SŪRAH YĀ SĪN

Text, Translation and Commentary

Compiled From Various Sources

Islamic Book Trust
Kuala Lumpur

Revised edition 2007
Reprint 2011

Published by
Islamic Book Trust
607 Mutiara Majestic
Jalan Othman
46000 Petaling Jaya
Selangor, Malaysia
www.ibtbooks.com

Islamic Book Trust is affiliated with The Other Press.

Perpustakaan Negara Malaysia Cataloguing-in-Publication Data

Surah Ya Sin : text, translation and commentary : compiled by various sources.
Bibliography: p. 139
ISBN 978-983-9154-67-2
1. Koran, Surah Yaa Sin--Criticism, Interpretation, etc. 2. Islam--Prayers and devotions.
297.1229

Printed by
Academe Art & Printing Services Sdn. Bhd.
7, Jalan Rajawali 1A, Bandar Puchong Jaya,
Batu 8, Jalan Puchong, 47100 Selangor.

NOTE FROM THE PUBLISHER

This is the fourth book published by Islamic Book Trust, focusing on individual Sūrahs of the Qur'an. The others in this series are *The Opening Chapter of the Qur'an*, an exegesis of Sūrah al-Fātiḥah, *The Prophet Joseph in the Qur'an, the Bible, and History* (Sūrah Yūsuf), and *Faith Versus Materialism* (Sūrah al-Kahf).

Sūrah Yā Sīn is often referred to as the "heart of the Qur'an". It is a Sūrah frequently recited from memory by a great majority of the Muslims on solemn occasions throughout the Muslim world. It is therefore incumbent upon us to know the meaning of the verses and their significance to derive maximum benefits from our recitation.

This book is mainly based on a small book under the title *From the Guidance of Surah Ya Seen*. It was a *tafsīr* compiled from Arabic sources and translated by Umm Muhammad. We have kept the *tafsīr* part of the book unchanged but simplified our Introduction to make it concise so that extraneous matters do not impinge upon the meaning of the Sūrah as it should be understood by ordinary intelligent people.

We wish to acknowledge our indebtedness to the original publishers Abul-Qasim Publishing House, Jeddah.

Sister Umm Muhammad, has done a great service to non-Arabic speaking Muslims all over the world by compiling and translating the *tafsīr* in English. May Allah *subḥānahu wa ta'ālā* reward her for her efforts.

Islamic Book Trust,
Kuala Lumpur
January 2007

CONTENTS

The Study of the Qur'an	ix
Introduction	1
Āyahs 1–12	3
Āyahs 13–32	31
Āyahs 33–44	55
Āyahs 45–54	75
Āyahs 55–68	91
Āyahs 69–83	112
References	139

بِسْمِ ٱللَّهِ ٱلرَّحْمَٰنِ ٱلرَّحِيمِ

THE STUDY OF THE QUR'AN

'Abdullah bin 'Umar bin al-Khaṭṭāb said, "We lived a long period[1] in which one was given *īmān* before the Qur'an, so (as it was being revealed) he would learn everything in it. Then I saw men who were given the Qur'an before *īmān*. One would read it from al-Fātiḥah to the end and would not know what it contained, reading it a reading of the worst quality."

The reading and recitation of the Qur'an is an important form of worship for which a Muslim can expect reward and benefit in the Hereafter. In fact, the definition of the Qur'an, which can be applied to no other book or speech, is "the words of Allah (ﷻ) revealed to Muḥammad (ﷺ), the recitation of which is a form of worship."[2]

There was a definite purpose behind the strong encouragement given by the Prophet (ﷺ) in many authentic *ḥadīths* for the recitation of the Qur'an, which has unfortunately been overlooked and forgotten by a majority of today's Muslims. That purpose is clearly stated in the Qur'an itself:

---

1. He refers here to the years during which the revelation was yet incomplete.
2. *Mabāḥith fī 'Ulūm al-Qur'ān*, p. 21.

كِتَٰبٌ أَنزَلْنَٰهُ إِلَيْكَ مُبَٰرَكٌ لِّيَدَّبَّرُوٓا۟ ءَايَٰتِهِۦ وَلِيَتَذَكَّرَ
أُو۟لُوا۟ ٱلْأَلْبَٰبِ ﴿٢٩﴾ ﴿ص﴾

A blessed Book We have revealed to you that they might contemplate its verses and that those of intellect would be reminded. (38:29)

أَفَلَا يَتَدَبَّرُونَ ٱلْقُرْءَانَ أَمْ عَلَىٰ قُلُوبٍ أَقْفَالُهَآ ﴿٢٤﴾ ﴿محمد﴾

Then do they not reflect upon the Qur'an? Or are there locks upon their hearts? (47:24)

أَفَلَا يَتَدَبَّرُونَ ٱلْقُرْءَانَ ۚ وَلَوْ كَانَ مِنْ عِندِ غَيْرِ ٱللَّهِ
لَوَجَدُوا۟ فِيهِ ٱخْتِلَٰفًا كَثِيرًا ﴿٨٢﴾ ﴿النساء﴾

Then do they not reflect upon the Qur'an? If it had been from (any) other than Allah, they would have found within it much contradiction. (4:82)

Shaykh al-Islam Aḥmad bin Taymiyyah has pointed out in his *Fatāwā* that even the ordinary words of men are spoken or written with the aim of being understood by the listener or reader and that the Qur'an is surely more worthy to be understood than the words of men.

There are degrees of understanding in relation to the Qur'an, they are:

1. That which is known only to Allah (ﷻ).
2. That which is known to scholars who have specialized.
3. That which is clear to everyone, even in translation—

> this is the law (*ie.,* ordinance and prohibition) about which there can be no excuse for ignorance and the knowledge of which is an obligation upon every Muslim, male and female.

No person can afford to be ignorant of the Qur'an, for it is the constitution revealed by Allah to regulate and govern human life. It contains important information about human destiny and that of the individual. It educates and raises men to the highest moral, intellectual and social level when they strive to comprehend it and apply its teachings to life. The early Islamic community succeeded because people did not approach the Book merely for the purpose of lively discussion, obtaining "culture", or emotional satisfaction. They approached it with the intention of learning what the Creator had prescribed for them in every situation so that they might act upon this information in the very best way possible. When the heart is receptive to the guidance of Allah, one will come to the Qur'an not simply in an emotional or academic manner, but with a sense of instruction for obedience and action. Without guidance, life is lived in animal indifference, but when purpose and direction become evident, man asserts his humanity. This assertion and effort toward the acceptance of Allah is what is called Islam.

A word about *tafsīr*

Since the Qur'an was revealed in the language of the Prophet's contemporaries, most of its meanings were naturally and immediately understood by them linguistically. *tafsīr* (explanation) became a necessity as Islam spread to more distant lands, taking in new peoples not as familiar with the Arabic language. It was undertaken for two principal reasons; first, to assist the understanding of those non-Arab peoples, and second, to guard against any change that might occur in the original interpretations with the passing of time.

As to how the Qur'an is explained, scholars have used certain criteria, mentioned briefly as follows:

1. The best and most certain way is through the Qur'an itself. Often another verse can be found similar in meaning to the one in question or giving further details about it.

2. If the meaning is not found within the text of the Qur'an, the next source is the *sunnah. Tafsīr* actually began during the time of revelation, when the *ṣaḥābah* (companions) would ask questions to clarify a point and the Prophet (ﷺ) would explain to them. These explanations were recorded and passed on to us in the form of *aḥādīth,* and their validity is confirmed by Allah, Who said: وَمَا يَنطِقُ عَنِ الْهَوَىٰ "And he does not speak from his own inclination" (53:3). Ibn Taymiyyah has added that the Prophet (ﷺ) taught his companions the meanings of the Qur'an, as well as its pronunciation, because Allah's statement: لَتُبَيِّنُنَّهُ لِلنَّاسِ "... that you should make it clear to the people" (3:187) includes both.

3. If no explanation was found in either the Qur'an or *ḥadīth,* scholars turned to that of the *ṣaḥābah* because they were the most familiar with each *āyah*—the time, place and immediate circumstances in which it was revealed. When they memorized a verse, they would not go on to another until they had fully understood it and applied it to their daily lives. Besides the four rightly guided *khalīfahs*, the most knowledgeable of the *ṣaḥābah* about the Qur'an were Ibn 'Abbās and Ibn Mas'ūd, followed by Ubayy bin Ka'b, Zayd bin Thābit, Abū Mūsā al-Ash'arī, 'Abdullah bin al-Zubayr, Anas bin Mālik, Abū Hurayrah, 'Abdullah bin 'Amr bin al-'Āṣ and Jābir bin 'Abdullah al-Anṣārī.
4. The last source for reference is the *tābi'ūn* (followers), who were students of the *ṣaḥābah* and took their knowledge from them but not directly from the Prophet (ﷺ) himself. According to Ibn Taymiyyah, the most knowledgeable of these were from Makkah since they were closest to Ibn 'Abbās. They included the following: Mujāhid, 'Atā' bin Abī Rabāḥ, 'Ikrimah, Ṭāwūs and Sa'īd bin Jubayr. In Kūfah were concentrated students of Ibn Mas'ūd: 'Alqamah, al-Aswad bin Yazīd, Ibrāhīm al-Nakha'ī, al-Sha'bī, al-Ḥasan al-Baṣrī, 'Aṭā', Qutādah and others. And in Madīnah were students of Ubayy bin Ka'b: Zayd bin Aslam, his son 'Abdul-Raḥmān and Mālik bin Anas.

The *tābi'ūn* always gave the sources for their *tafsīrs*. For example, Mujāhid said, "I went over the Qur'an three times with Ibn 'Abbās from beginning to end, stopping at the end of every *āyah* and asking him about it."

The question often arises: How does one accept the differences among these early scholars in their explanations? Actually, most of their differences were simply variations rather than contradicting views, each containing a truth or one side of a truth.[3] Some commentaries included information taken from Jewish sources (*isrā'īliyyāt*) for the purpose of filling in further detail, but these narrations were not meant to be considered as fact. For the Prophet (ﷺ) had said, "Neither believe the People of the Scriptures[4] nor disbelieve them, but say, 'We believe in Allah and what has been revealed to us.'"[5]

5. Conclusions reached by *ijtihād* (sincere efforts to find the correct meaning according to accepted

---

3. An example has been given by Ibn Taymiyyah in the verse:

﴿ٱهْدِنَا ٱلصِّرَٰطَ ٱلْمُسْتَقِيمَ ۝٦﴾ ﴿الفاتحة﴾

"Guide us to the straight way" (1:6). Commentators have asserted that "the straight way" means: 1. Islam, 2. following the Book of Allah, 3. the way of the *sunnah* and its adherents, 4. the path of worship, 5. acting in obedience to Allah, and 6. following the Qur'an and the *sunnah*. In essence, all are descriptions of the same thing, so one cannot say that any one of them is wrong.

4. *ie.,* the Jews and Christians.

5. Al-Bukhārī.

> methods) are permissible as long as they are not contrary to those based on the aforementioned criteria or to actual reality or to the literal and logical meanings understood in the Arabic language. It is absolutely forbidden, however, for anyone to explain the Qur'an by personal opinions or current theories. The Prophet (ﷺ) is reported to have said, "Whoever says something about the Qur'an according to his own opinion or without knowledge—let him take his seat in the Hellfire."[6]

Ibn Taymiyyah has warned against the acceptance of any *tafsīrs* contrary to the *sunnah* or of those including innovations in religion, as well as those of sects, groups or individuals seeking to use the Qur'an to support their own beliefs or who consider that its meanings "change with the times". All of these are prone to misinterpretation.

A natural extension of *tafsīr* is the translation of the Qur'an's meanings into other languages.[7] The same caution should be observed, however, in relation to these translations and commentaries, and all statements must be subjected to the criteria stipulated for Arabic *tafsīr*.

This book deals with the study of Sūrah Yā Sīn. It is based principally upon three *tafsīrs* of Ibn Kathīr, al-

---

6. Al-Tirmidhī and al-Nasā'ī—*ḥasan*.
7. The Qur'an, as the words of Allah, can never be translated literally. Therefore, it is incorrect to use the term "translation of the Qur'an", since it is actually only a *tafsīr* (an explanation of the meanings).

Qurṭubī and Sayyid Quṭb, and out of those, care has been taken to avoid any questionable interpretations. Although it will necessarily fall short of an Arabic *tafsīr,* this book is an attempt to bring the reader into the atmosphere of the Sūrah and facilitate his understanding of its meanings. Seeking refuge from Shayṭān, we ask Allah's guidance and acceptance in all endeavors.

INTRODUCTION

Sūrah Yā Sīn is the thirty sixth chapter of the Qur'an. Revealed in the early part of what is termed the "middle" Makkan period (probably) just before al-Fūrqān, this Sūrah considered the "heart of the Qur'an" as it is entirely devoted to the problem of man's moral responsibility and, hence, to the certainty of Resurrection and Allah's judgement; and it is for this reason that the Prophet (ﷺ) called upon his followers to recite it over the dying and in prayers for the dead.

Several *ḥadīths* are often quoted in connection with Sūrah Yā Sīn. Although none are classified as *ṣaḥīḥ,* perhaps the most accepted among them is that narrated by Aḥmad, Abū Dāwūd, al-Nasā'ī and Ibn Mājah in which Ma'qil bin Yasār reported that the Messenger of Allah (ﷺ) said, اقرؤوها على موتاكم "Recite it over your dying ones", meaning Yā Sīn.

In Arabic, the word *mawtā* is used according to specific contexts to mean either "dying" or "dead". The first meaning in this case is supported by another *ḥadīth* which uses the same word: لقنوا موتاكم لا إله الا الله "Help your dying ones to say, *Lā ilāha illa-Allāh*".[1] Obviously, this could not apply to the dead but only to those on the verge

1. Muslim, Abū Dāwūd and al-Tirmidhī.

of death. Imām Aḥmad mentioned that the scholars used to say, "When Yā Sīn is read for the dying, Allah eases it for him by that." By this he meant that Allah makes the exit of the soul easier, just as recitation of the Sūrah is said to ease any difficult matter. But, as in all affairs, it is Allah Who knows best.

Indeed, there is no doubt that reading or recitation at any time benefits the reader and would also be comforting to the family of the deceased. What is objectionable, however, is the stipulation of certain conditions as to when and how it must be done, turning it into a ritual. Thus, one should concentrate on supplication for the deceased or charity on his behalf, about which there is no doubt and which is encouraged in the *sunnah.* May Allah guide us and cover us with His mercy both in life and death.

بِسۡمِ ٱللَّهِ ٱلرَّحۡمَٰنِ ٱلرَّحِيمِ

ĀYAHS 1–12

يسٓ ﴿١﴾ وَٱلۡقُرۡءَانِ ٱلۡحَكِيمِ ﴿٢﴾ إِنَّكَ لَمِنَ ٱلۡمُرۡسَلِينَ ﴿٣﴾ عَلَىٰ
صِرَٰطٖ مُّسۡتَقِيمٖ ﴿٤﴾ تَنزِيلَ ٱلۡعَزِيزِ ٱلرَّحِيمِ ﴿٥﴾ لِتُنذِرَ قَوۡمٗا مَّآ
أُنذِرَ ءَابَآؤُهُمۡ فَهُمۡ غَٰفِلُونَ ﴿٦﴾ لَقَدۡ حَقَّ ٱلۡقَوۡلُ عَلَىٰٓ أَكۡثَرِهِمۡ فَهُمۡ
لَا يُؤۡمِنُونَ ﴿٧﴾ إِنَّا جَعَلۡنَا فِيٓ أَعۡنَٰقِهِمۡ أَغۡلَٰلٗا فَهِيَ إِلَى ٱلۡأَذۡقَانِ
فَهُم مُّقۡمَحُونَ ﴿٨﴾ وَجَعَلۡنَا مِنۢ بَيۡنِ أَيۡدِيهِمۡ سَدّٗا وَمِنۡ خَلۡفِهِمۡ
سَدّٗا فَأَغۡشَيۡنَٰهُمۡ فَهُمۡ لَا يُبۡصِرُونَ ﴿٩﴾ وَسَوَآءٌ عَلَيۡهِمۡ ءَأَنذَرۡتَهُمۡ أَمۡ
لَمۡ تُنذِرۡهُمۡ لَا يُؤۡمِنُونَ ﴿١٠﴾ إِنَّمَا تُنذِرُ مَنِ ٱتَّبَعَ ٱلذِّكۡرَ وَخَشِيَ
ٱلرَّحۡمَٰنَ بِٱلۡغَيۡبِۖ فَبَشِّرۡهُ بِمَغۡفِرَةٖ وَأَجۡرٖ كَرِيمٍ ﴿١١﴾ إِنَّا نَحۡنُ نُحۡيِ
ٱلۡمَوۡتَىٰ وَنَكۡتُبُ مَا قَدَّمُواْ وَءَاثَٰرَهُمۡۚ وَكُلَّ شَيۡءٍ أَحۡصَيۡنَٰهُ فِيٓ إِمَامٖ
مُّبِينٖ ﴿١٢﴾

[1] Yā Sīn [2] By the wise Qur'an, [3] Certainly you are from among the messengers, [4] On a straight path. [5] A revelation of the Mighty, the Merciful, [6] That you may warn a people whose forefathers were not warned, so they are unaware. [7] Already the Word has come into

effect upon most of them, so they do not believe. [8]
Indeed, We have put shackles around their necks, which
are up to their chins, so their heads are kept aloft. [9]
And We have put before them a barrier and behind them
a barrier and covered them so they do not see. [10] And
it is all the same to them whether you warn them or do
not warn them—they will not believe. [11] You can only
warn one who follows the Remembrance and fears al-Raḥmān unseen. So give him good tidings of forgiveness
and of generous reward. [12] It is We Who bring the
dead to life and record what they have put forth and left
behind, and all things We have enumerated in a clear
register.

In the Name of Allah, Most Gracious, Most Merciful

Allah (ﷻ) begins in His own name—that proper name belonging only to the one Almighty God, creator and sustainer of mankind and of all creation. Because the name "Allah" is inclusive of all of His descriptive names, it is said to be the greatest of His names, and nothing other than Him has ever been called "Allah". The phrase *Bismillāh* has been explained by students of grammar as being an abbreviation, its complete meaning understood in context as: "I begin in the name of Allah." Ibn 'Abbās stated that the Messenger of Allah (ﷺ) would not know where a Sūrah ended and the next one began until the revelation to him of the words "*Bismillāh al-Raḥmān al-Raḥīm*".[1]

1. Abū Dāwūd—*Ṣaḥīh*.

Al-Raḥmān al-Raḥīm are two of Allah's descriptive names derived from the word *raḥmān* (mercy), both being intensive forms of "merciful" (*ie.,* extremely merciful). A double meaning is intended by using both together.

Raḥmān is used only to describe Allah, while *raḥīm* might be used to describe a person as well. The Prophet (ﷺ) was described in the Qur'an as *raḥīm. Raḥmān* is above and beyond the human capacity—intensely merciful. Lest intensity be understood as something of limited duration, Allah describes Himself further as *Raḥīm*—continually merciful.

Raḥmān also carries a wider and more general meaning—merciful to all creation. Justice is a part of this mercy. *Raḥīm* has a meaning of specificity—especially and specifically merciful to the believers. Forgiveness is a part of this mercy.[2]

Āyah 1

[1] Yā Sīn. يسٓ ۝١

These two letters, from which the Sūrah takes its name, are among the fourteen which occur in various combinations at the beginning of twenty-nine Sūrahs in the Qur'an. There has been much speculation as to the meanings of these opening letters, but, in reality, they belong to that category of *āyahs* about which true knowledge rests only with Allah. Since this is the case, some scholars have maintained that it is not permissible to try to explain them

2. See al-Qurṭubī's *Al-Jāmi' li Aḥkām al-Qur'ān,* pp. 103–107.

in any way. Others have submitted that they are among the proofs given by Allah (ﷻ) of the inimitability of the Qur'an since He has kept their purpose to Himself. They have noted that almost always the opening letters are followed by a reference to the Qur'an or the Book—as if a challenge to all humanity, which stands helpless to oppose divine scripture by producing anything similar to it. Human failure remains, in spite of the fact that this Book consists of the same phonetic symbols used by men who pride themselves on linguistic skill. Any assertion beyond this point as to actual meanings must be rejected as having no basis in the Qur'an or the *sunnah* of the Prophet (ﷺ).

Concerning this *āyah* in particular, it has been stated that Yā Sīn is a name designated to Allah's Messenger (ﷺ) because the third *āyah* (following an oath) addresses him directly. Other theories hold that the letters represent a name of Allah or carry the meaning: "O mankind" (*yā insān*). Again there is no proof for any of these statements, and one can only attribute certain knowledge to their author, Allah, the Exalted.

Āyahs 2–3

وَٱلْقُرْءَانِ ٱلْحَكِيمِ ۝٢ إِنَّكَ لَمِنَ ٱلْمُرْسَلِينَ ۝٣

[2] By the wise Qur'an, [3] Certainly you are from among the messengers.

Allah (ﷻ) swears by the Qur'an, full of wisdom. The letter *wāw* (و), which translates here as "by", is understood to stand for the phrase "I swear by" and designates an oath. While it is unacceptable that a man should take an oath except in the name of Allah,[3] He may swear by whatever He wills, be it Himself, His creations, His signs or His revelation.

An oath is a means of confirmation or removing doubt from the mind. The Qur'an was revealed to all people, among them those who accept truth readily, those who doubt and hesitate, and those who deny. The oath, when used by Allah (ﷻ), serves to erase all doubts, clarify any questions, establish evidence and confirm information absolutely.

The Qur'an is described as *ḥakīm* (wise), and this is an adjective normally used for an intelligent being. Thus, the words of Allah are characterized with the qualities of life, will, purpose and discrimination, which are essential to wisdom. *Ḥakīm* also carries the meaning of having been made precise or exact—that which neither contains any fault or contradiction nor is subject to change. The Qur'an speaks with the perfect knowledge of the Creator about His creation. It teaches with wisdom and establishes the best system of life for humanity.

One is immediately alerted by an oath from Allah (ﷻ) that a most important statement is to follow—the object of His concern.

Allah (ﷻ) swears in order to remove any and all misgivings about the prophethood of Muḥammad (ﷺ),

---

3. 'Umar bin al-Khaṭṭāb reported that the Messenger of Allah (ﷺ) said, "Whoever swears by other than Allah has disbelieved or committed *shirk* (association with Him)." Al-Tirmidhī considered it *ḥasan;* al-Ḥākim graded it *ṣaḥīḥ*.

stating categorically and directly to him: "Certainly you, (O Muḥammad), are from among the messengers."[4] The statement assumes the acceptance by the people of the fact that previous messengers were sent by Allah to mankind, and it goes on to confirm that Muḥammad (ﷺ) is surely one of them. This essential point of faith is one of the main subjects of Makkan Sūrahs and is picked up again near the end of this Sūrah in *āyah* 69. Sayyid Quṭb has drawn attention to the fact that in the present *āyah,* Allah (ﷻ) addresses His prophet directly rather than the people, showing that the subject of his prophethood is a truth not to be discussed or argued with them. Rather, it is established and confirmed by Him, irrespective of their opinions.

Ibn 'Abbās related that the disbelievers of Quraysh confronted the Prophet (ﷺ), saying, "You are not, O Muḥammad, a messenger, and Allah has not sent you to us." In this verse Allah (ﷻ) refutes this statement, swearing by the great and precise Qur'an that Muḥammad (ﷺ) was indeed from the messengers.[5]

Āyah 4

[4] On a straight path. عَلَىٰ صِرَٰطٍ مُّسْتَقِيمٍ ﴿٤﴾

On a straight and direct path, which is defined by Allah and explained by all of His messengers—the way of submission to His will:

---

4. The word *mursal* (singular of *mursalīn)* literally means "one who is sent". *Rasūl* is also used for "messenger".
5. Recorded by al-Qurṭubī in his *tafsīr.*

صِرَٰطِ ٱللَّهِ ٱلَّذِى لَهُۥ مَا فِى ٱلسَّمَـٰوَٰتِ وَمَا فِى ٱلْأَرْضِ ۗ أَلَآ إِلَى ٱللَّهِ تَصِيرُ ٱلْأُمُورُ ﴿٥٣﴾ ﴿الشورى﴾

"The path of Allah to Whom belongs the heavens and earth ..." (42:53)

Al-ṣirāṭ al-mustaqīm (the straight path) is further explained in Sūrah al-Fātiḥah as:

صِرَٰطَ ٱلَّذِينَ أَنْعَمْتَ عَلَيْهِمْ غَيْرِ ٱلْمَغْضُوبِ عَلَيْهِمْ وَلَا ٱلضَّآلِّينَ ﴿٧﴾ ﴿الفاتحة﴾

"The way of those whom You have blessed, not of those who have evoked (Your) anger nor of those who have gone astray." (1:7)

The nature of this message brought by all prophets is uprightness and straightforwardness. Its truth is clear with no obscurity and no supposition, bending neither with human whims nor with temporary worldly interests—direct, uncomplicated and in harmony with the nature of man and his surroundings.

In describing the "straight path", various commentators have designated its meanings as Islam, the *sunnah* of the Prophet (ﷺ), following the Book of Allah, the path of worship, obedience to Allah, and acting in accordance with the Qur'an and the *sunnah.* All of these are essentially the same and are correct.[6]

6. *Fatāwā Ibn Taymiyyah.*

Āyahs 5–6

تَنزِيلَ ٱلْعَزِيزِ ٱلرَّحِيمِ ﴿٥﴾ لِتُنذِرَ قَوْمًا مَّآ أُنذِرَ ءَابَآؤُهُمْ
فَهُمْ غَـٰفِلُونَ ﴿٦﴾

[5] A revelation of the Mighty, the Merciful, [6] That you may warn a people whose forefathers were not warned so they are unaware.

This revelation,[7] the Qur'an, is the guide for those who seek to follow the Straight Path. It has been sent down to mankind by *al-'Azīz*, the One Who has power over all things and could certainly have forced all men to submit to His will in Islam if He had so chosen. And yet, He is also *al-Raḥīm*, especially merciful (beyond His general mercy to all creatures) to those who believe in Him and who follow His guidance.

Muḥammad bin 'Abdullah (ﷺ) was raised among a people who had known no other prophet since the time of Ismā'īl (عليه السلام). Although they had not completely forgotten Allah, the Arabs worshipped Him superficially, usually associating man-made deities with Him, calling upon them in supplication and obeying only the law of their own desires and corrupted customs.

Although Prophet Muḥammad (ﷺ) was sent to the whole of mankind, he naturally had to begin his invitation

7. The word *tanzīl*, literally, "a sending down", is derived from *nazzala*, meaning "to let down bit by bit". This is opposed to *anzala*, which means "to let down all at once".

to Allah with his own people and initially within his own family. Ibn 'Abbās related that when Allah (ﷻ) revealed the *āyah*:

﴿ وَأَنذِرْ عَشِيرَتَكَ ٱلْأَقْرَبِينَ ۝٢١٤ ﴾ ﴿الشعراء﴾

"And warn your nearest kinsmen." (26:214)

The Prophet (ﷺ) mounted al-Ṣafā, calling out to assemble the people, and then said to them, "Would you believe me if I informed you that (enemy) horses were atop the mountain waiting to attack?" "Yes", they replied. He said, "Then believe that I am a warner to you of a severe punishment to come!" At that, his uncle, Abū Lahab, snapped, "Is it for this that you have gathered us?! May you have loss and destruction all day long." At that, Allah (ﷻ) revealed:

﴿ تَبَّتْ يَدَآ أَبِى لَهَبٍ وَتَبَّ ۝١ ﴾ ﴿المسد﴾

"May the hands of Abū Lahab be destroyed, and destroyed is he ..." to the end of Sūrah al-Masad.[8]

Additionally, when the aforementioned *āyah* (26:214) was revealed, 'Ā'ishah reported that the Prophet (ﷺ) arose and said, "O Fāṭimah, daughter of Muḥammad! O Ṣafiyyah, daughter of 'Abdul-Muṭṭalib! O sons of 'Abdul-Muṭṭalib! I cannot avail you before Allah at all, but you can ask me of my property what you wish."[9] And Abū Hurayrah reported that he called out, "O people of Quraysh,

8. Al-Bukhārī, Muslim, al-Tirmidhī and al-Nasā'ī. The Qur'anic reference is Sūrah al-Masad, (111:1).
9. Muslim and Aḥmad.

save yourselves from the Fire! O people of Banī Ka'b, save yourselves from the Fire! O people of Banī Hāshim, save yourselves from the Fire! O people of 'Abdul-Muṭṭalib, save yourselves from the Fire! O Fāṭimah, daughter of Muḥammad, save yourself from the Fire!"[10]

There is no doubt that the message of Islam was never meant to be limited to the Arabs. The Prophet (ﷺ) made it clear that he was sent to all mankind—black and white, Arab and non-Arab. He sent messages of warning and invitation to Islam to the rulers of neighboring nations and empires. In the Qur'an, Allah ordered him to say:

قُلْ يَٰٓأَيُّهَا ٱلنَّاسُ إِنِّى رَسُولُ ٱللَّهِ إِلَيْكُمْ جَمِيعًا ٱلَّذِى لَهُۥ مُلْكُ
ٱلسَّمَٰوَٰتِ وَٱلْأَرْضِ ۖ لَآ إِلَٰهَ إِلَّا هُوَ يُحْىِۦ وَيُمِيتُ ۖ فَـَٔامِنُوا۟ بِٱللَّهِ
وَرَسُولِهِ ٱلنَّبِىِّ ٱلْأُمِّىِّ ٱلَّذِى يُؤْمِنُ بِٱللَّهِ وَكَلِمَٰتِهِۦ وَٱتَّبِعُوهُ
لَعَلَّكُمْ تَهْتَدُونَ ﴿١٥٨﴾ ﴿الأعراف﴾

"Say (O Muḥammad): O people, truly I am the messenger of Allah to all of you ..." (7:158)

Furthermore, He stated:

وَمَآ أَرْسَلْنَٰكَ إِلَّا كَآفَّةً لِّلنَّاسِ بَشِيرًا وَنَذِيرًا وَلَٰكِنَّ أَكْثَرَ
ٱلنَّاسِ لَا يَعْلَمُونَ ﴿٢٨﴾ ﴿سبأ﴾

"And We have not sent you except inclusively to all the people as a giver of good tidings and a warner ..." (34:28)[11]

---

10. Muslim, Aḥmad and al-Tirmidhī.
11. *Kāffah* literally means "inclusively, without exception".

Unawareness (*ghaflah*) is a serious ailment of the heart, blocking its natural function of reception and response to truth and righteousness. It often takes a shock of some sort to initiate an awakening, and an appropriate treatment for a people unaware of the consequences of their behavior is a warning that they are in danger.

Āyah 7

لَقَدْ حَقَّ ٱلْقَوْلُ عَلَىٰٓ أَكْثَرِهِمْ فَهُمْ لَا يُؤْمِنُونَ ﴿٧﴾

[7] Already the Word has come into effect upon most of them, so they do not believe.

"The Word" here refers to the decree of Allah (ﷻ)—very likely the same that is mentioned in Sūrah al-Sajdah:

وَلَوْ شِئْنَا لَـَٔاتَيْنَا كُلَّ نَفْسٍ هُدَىٰهَا وَلَـٰكِنْ حَقَّ ٱلْقَوْلُ مِنِّى لَأَمْلَأَنَّ جَهَنَّمَ مِنَ ٱلْجِنَّةِ وَٱلنَّاسِ أَجْمَعِينَ ﴿١٣﴾ ﴿السجدة﴾

"... Certainly shall I fill Hellfire with jinn and men all together." (32:13)[12]

It is an indication of Allah's knowledge that most of the people who first heard the divine message would reject it and die in a state of disbelief, thereby bringing punishment upon themselves. This is because He is fully aware of all aspects of His servants' natures, attitudes and potentials, and He knows with certainty what will be the response of each soul to the Prophet's warnings.

---

12. See *Tafsīr al-Nasafī* concerning this *āyah*. *Al-qawl* literally means "speech or saying". See also Sūrah Hūd, (11:119).

It should not be taken to mean, however, that they were "helpless victims of divine decree," as the fatalists would have us believe, for Allah's knowledge of what will be in the future in no way implies that He compels one to a certain direction or deprives him of freedom and thus of responsibility. Exalted is He above any such injustice!

In reality, Allah (ﷻ) has willed for mankind (and for the *jinn* as well) freedom of choice in matters of belief and in many decisions concerning various courses of action open to the individual. Man is taken to account only for that which is subject to his control, so those who die without having incurred responsibility (*ie.,* young children or the mentally deficient) are exempted of blame.[13] Whenever human will is impaired, responsibility diminishes. Therefore, Allah (ﷻ) has not ordered anything that man does not have the ability to carry out, and He has not prohibited anything that he is helpless to avoid. And since man himself is unaware of his own future and of his destination in the Hereafter, it cannot be said that divine knowledge has any effect upon the decisions he makes during his lifetime. When the Prophet (ﷺ) was asked whether there was any use in performing deeds since one's place in Heaven or Hell has already been decreed, he answered,

---

13. The Prophet (ﷺ) said, "The pen has been lifted (*ie.,* does not register) for three: the sleeping one until he awakens, the boy until he reaches puberty, and the insane until he becomes sane" (Al-Bukhārī and Muslim). And he also said, "My community has been excused for (unintended) mistakes, forgetting, and that which has been forced upon it" (Ibn Mājah and al-Ṭabarānī—*ṣaḥīḥ*).

"Work. For everyone is eased toward that for which he was created." Then he recited:

فَأَمَّا مَنْ أَعْطَىٰ وَٱتَّقَىٰ ۝٥ وَصَدَّقَ بِٱلْحُسْنَىٰ ۝٦ فَسَنُيَسِّرُهُۥ لِلْيُسْرَىٰ ۝٧ وَأَمَّا مَنۢ بَخِلَ وَٱسْتَغْنَىٰ ۝٨ وَكَذَّبَ بِٱلْحُسْنَىٰ ۝٩ فَسَنُيَسِّرُهُۥ لِلْعُسْرَىٰ ۝١٠ ﴿الليل﴾

"Those who give, are conscious (of Allah), and believe in the good reward—We shall ease them towards ease. But as for those who withhold (what they have), consider themselves self-sufficient, and deny the good reward—We shall ease them towards difficulty." (92:5–10)

Ibn Kathīr has pointed out that when one intends righteousness, Allah rewards him by helping him to realize it. And when he intends evil, Allah leaves him to his own devices.

Certain words of the Prophet (ﷺ), although clearly perceived by his contemporaries, have been grossly misunderstood by later generations. They are part of an authentic *ḥadīth* related by Ibn Mas'ūd about creation within the womb—how the angel blows a soul into the fetus and is then ordered to write down four decrees concerning that person: his provision and sustenance on earth, his life span, his deeds, and whether he will ultimately he happy or unhappy (in the Hereafter). "By Allah, other than Whom there is no deity," the Prophet (ﷺ) said, "indeed, one of you may do the deeds of the people of Paradise until he is only an arm's length away and then is overtaken by the decree, so he does the deeds of the people of the Fire and enters it. And one of you may do the deeds of the people of the Fire until he is only an arm's length away and then is overtaken by the decree, so he does the deeds of the people of Paradise and enters it."[14]

There are several points to be clarified concerning this *ḥadīth*:

1. It refers to a possibility. One might or could do as mentioned therein, but in the usual pattern of human behavior it is recognized that men do not suddenly change at the end of life—although it does happen occasionally.[15]
2. Allah does not judge a person solely according to His own divine knowledge; otherwise, it could be claimed that there is no evidence to convict the guilty. A student would not readily accept the judgement of his teacher that he had failed a course in which he had not been permitted to take the required examinations. Evidence can be brought justly against (or in favor of) a particular soul only by its own witness and by that of others concerning actual occurrences.
3. The fact that a person who has lived a life of wrongdoing or disbelief can repent and change himself even in his last days, thereby gaining forgiveness and entrance into Paradise, points to the great generosity of Allah in His acceptance of such a servant, and it shows that one should never despair of His mercy.

---

14. Al-Bukhārī and Muslim.
15. See al-Nawawī's explanation of the *ḥadīth* in *Ṣaḥīḥ Muslim*.

4. The case given of the opposite possibility (*ie.,* of one entering Hellfire after having lived most of his life in righteousness) is a warning to every believer to be on guard against such an occurrence. Just as one is capable of changing from evil to good and is rewarded for that, he is also responsible for keeping himself on the right path by not depending upon past deeds as sufficient for him and consequently relaxing his discipline. And further, by intending and continuing to work hard for the acceptance of Allah—seeking His assistance in this goal up until the very last breaths of his life—he will die in a state which is pleasing to his Creator. We ask Allah to make the best of our deeds the final ones.

Predestination (*qadar*) is an article of faith. All things are predestined by Allah, Who says:

﴿وَمَا تَشَآءُونَ إِلَّآ أَن يَشَآءَ ٱللَّهُۚ إِنَّ ٱللَّهَ كَانَ عَلِيمًا حَكِيمًا ٣٠﴾ ﴿الإنسان﴾

"And you do not will except that Allah wills ..." (76:30)

This means that Allah wills that one must make a choice in particular matters. He knows beforehand what the servant will choose, and He wills whatever choice is made by that servant, whether right or wrong. The choice itself is made freely and without compulsion from Allah. Thus human responsibility is established.

There are those who claim that if Allah wills a thing, then He must approve of it. But they are mistaken—for what He wills and what He likes are not necessarily the same. By way of example:

وَقَٰتِلُواْ فِي سَبِيلِ ٱللَّهِ ٱلَّذِينَ يُقَٰتِلُونَكُمۡ وَلَا تَعۡتَدُوٓاْۚ إِنَّ ٱللَّهَ لَا يُحِبُّ ٱلۡمُعۡتَدِينَ ﴿١٩٠﴾ ﴿البقرة﴾

"… Certainly Allah does not like aggressors." (2:190)

وَإِذَا تَوَلَّىٰ سَعَىٰ فِي ٱلۡأَرۡضِ لِيُفۡسِدَ فِيهَا وَيُهۡلِكَ ٱلۡحَرۡثَ وَٱلنَّسۡلَۗ وَٱللَّهُ لَا يُحِبُّ ٱلۡفَسَادَ ﴿٢٠٥﴾ ﴿البقرة﴾

"… And Allah does not like corruption." (2:205)

قُلۡ أَطِيعُواْ ٱللَّهَ وَٱلرَّسُولَۖ فَإِن تَوَلَّوۡاْ فَإِنَّ ٱللَّهَ لَا يُحِبُّ ٱلۡكَٰفِرِينَ ﴿٣٢﴾ ﴿آل عمران﴾

"… Allah does not like the disbelievers." (3:32)

وَأَمَّا ٱلَّذِينَ ءَامَنُواْ وَعَمِلُواْ ٱلصَّٰلِحَٰتِ فَيُوَفِّيهِمۡ أُجُورَهُمۡۗ وَٱللَّهُ لَا يُحِبُّ ٱلظَّٰلِمِينَ ﴿٥٧﴾ ﴿آل عمران﴾

"… And Allah does not like the unjust." (3:57)

۞ يَٰبَنِيٓ ءَادَمَ خُذُواْ زِينَتَكُمۡ عِندَ كُلِّ مَسۡجِدٖ وَكُلُواْ وَٱشۡرَبُواْ وَلَا تُسۡرِفُوٓاْۚ إِنَّهُۥ لَا يُحِبُّ ٱلۡمُسۡرِفِينَ ﴿٣١﴾ ﴿الأعراف﴾

"… He does not like the extravagant." (7:31)

وَإِمَّا تَخَافَنَّ مِن قَوۡمٍ خِيَانَةٗ فَٱنۢبِذۡ إِلَيۡهِمۡ عَلَىٰ سَوَآءٍۚ إِنَّ ٱللَّهَ لَا يُحِبُّ ٱلۡخَآئِنِينَ ﴿٥٨﴾ ﴿الأنفال﴾

"… Indeed Allah does not like traitors." (8:58)

﴿لَا جَرَمَ أَنَّ ٱللَّهَ يَعْلَمُ مَا يُسِرُّونَ وَمَا يُعْلِنُونَ ۚ إِنَّهُۥ لَا يُحِبُّ ٱلْمُسْتَكْبِرِينَ ﴿٢٣﴾﴾ النحل

"... Indeed He does not like the arrogant." (16:23)

Allah (ﷻ) has willed the existence of all of these; yet, as the *āyahs* show, He does not like any of them. He has ordered belief in and obedience to Himself, yet He has also willed the occurrence of disbelief and disobedience, which anger Him. Concerning human choice, Allah (ﷻ) has accordingly made known His own pleasure or displeasure. He has issued warnings and sent guidance for all who would benefit.

As for those happenings beyond a servant's control, the believer can take comfort in the fact that they, too, are predestined and willed by the just and merciful Creator. Trusting that Allah knows best as to where true benefit lies, the servant can expect great reward for patience in hardship and difficulty:

﴿مَآ أَصَابَ مِن مُّصِيبَةٍ فِى ٱلْأَرْضِ وَلَا فِىٓ أَنفُسِكُمْ إِلَّا فِى كِتَٰبٍ مِّن قَبْلِ أَن نَّبْرَأَهَآ ۚ إِنَّ ذَٰلِكَ عَلَى ٱللَّهِ يَسِيرٌ ﴿٢٢﴾ لِّكَيْلَا تَأْسَوْا۟ عَلَىٰ مَا فَاتَكُمْ وَلَا تَفْرَحُوا۟ بِمَآ ءَاتَىٰكُمْ ۗ وَٱللَّهُ لَا يُحِبُّ كُلَّ مُخْتَالٍ فَخُورٍ ﴿٢٣﴾﴾ الحديد

"No misfortune strikes upon the earth or within yourselves except that it is in a register before We bring it into being. Indeed, that is easy for Allah. In order that you not despair over what has eluded you and not exult (in pride) over what He has given you ...” (57:22–23)

Āyah 8

إِنَّا جَعَلْنَا فِىٓ أَعْنَـٰقِهِمْ أَغْلَـٰلًا فَهِىَ إِلَى ٱلْأَذْقَانِ فَهُم مُّقْمَحُونَ ﴿٨﴾

> [8] Indeed We have put shackles around their necks, which are up to their chins, so their heads are kept aloft.

Allah (ﷻ) continues with a description of those who have deserved His decree against them. Their heads, held high in pride and disdain, have been locked into that position by shackles of stubbornness, which prevents them from submitting to the truth.

Aghlāl refers to a device used to restrain prisoners. It consists of an iron collar to which the hands are secured under the chin. Obviously, when confined in this position, one is unable to lower his head, even in humility to his Lord. Unable as well to see except in one direction, he cannot discover much of the truth around him, and with his hands chained to his neck, he cannot reach out to benefit anyone at all. Such is the prisoner of his own arrogance. Those whose heads are held up in this position are called *muqmaḥūn*. The same word is used for a camel which refuses to drink, stubbornly thrusting its head into the air.

The psychological state pictured so aptly in this and the following verses is an attitude of conceit, hard-heartedness and considering oneself superior. This type of personality will not accept guidance and, therefore, cannot be guided.

Āyah 9

وَجَعَلْنَا مِنۢ بَيْنِ أَيْدِيهِمْ سَدًّا وَمِنْ خَلْفِهِمْ سَدًّا فَأَغْشَيْنَٰهُمْ فَهُمْ لَا يُبْصِرُونَ ﴿٩﴾

> [9] And We have put before them a barrier and behind them barrier and covered them so they do not see.

The overall picture of total helplessness is now complete. Those who reject faith are confined by the barriers of their own prejudices and misconceptions, unable to benefit from lessons of the past or from the experience of the present. Blinded against truth and reality, they will never change their course. How dreadful is their condition!

'Ikrimah related that his father, Abū Jahl,[16] had threatened, "When I see Muḥammad, I am going to do this and that." Then Allah revealed: "Indeed, We have put shackles around their necks" up through the words "... so they do not see". They pointed out to him, "There is Muḥammad," but he could only say, "Where is he? Where is he? I do not see him!"

---

16. One of the Prophet's uncles, who was among the foremost enemies of Islam.

In his *sīrah* (biography of the Prophet) Ibn Hishām narrated that the leaders of Quraysh were assembled at night outside the house of the Prophet (ﷺ), awaiting the moment to carry out his assassination. But Allah had warned him of their plan. While they sat in wait, the Messenger of Allah came out. Taking a handful of earth and sprinkling it over the heads of the would-be assassins, he recited this *āyah*: “And We have put before them a barrier” to the end. Allah turned their vision away so that they did not see him, and there remained no man among them whose head was not covered with earth. Then the Prophet (ﷺ) passed by them and went on to the house of Abū Bakr, from which they escaped to the cave of Thawr.

Āyah 10

وَسَوَآءٌ عَلَيۡهِمۡ ءَأَنذَرۡتَهُمۡ أَمۡ لَمۡ تُنذِرۡهُمۡ لَا يُؤۡمِنُونَ ﴿١٠﴾

[10] And it is all the same to them whether you warn them or do not warn them—they will not believe.

These people are such that no warning can move their hearts. Here is a consolation for the Prophet (ﷺ), who was often saddened by his own people’s rejection of Allah’s message, and subsequently for those whose *da‘wah* efforts do not always bring the desired result. The denial of clear guidance by any servant is but a penalty for previous sins and attitudes that have reached a point of no return—where no hope for righteousness remains.

This cause and effect situation in which the servant uses his free will in a rebellious manner, thereby closing the door to his own salvation, is again illustrated in other *āyahs*:

فِي قُلُوبِهِم مَّرَضٌ فَزَادَهُمُ ٱللَّهُ مَرَضًا ۖ وَلَهُمْ عَذَابٌ أَلِيمٌۢ بِمَا كَانُوا۟
يَكْذِبُونَ ﴿١٠﴾ ﴿البقرة﴾

"There is illness in their hearts, so Allah has increased them in illness ..." (2:10)[17]

فَأَعْقَبَهُمْ نِفَاقًا فِي قُلُوبِهِمْ إِلَىٰ يَوْمِ يَلْقَوْنَهُۥ بِمَآ أَخْلَفُوا۟ ٱللَّهَ مَا
وَعَدُوهُ وَبِمَا كَانُوا۟ يَكْذِبُونَ ﴿٧٧﴾ ﴿التوبة﴾

"So He penalized them with hypocrisy in their hearts until the Day that they shall meet Him because they failed Allah in what they promised Him and because they (habitually) used to lie." (9:77)

وَإِذْ قَالَ مُوسَىٰ لِقَوْمِهِۦ يَٰقَوْمِ لِمَ تُؤْذُونَنِي وَقَد تَّعْلَمُونَ أَنِّي
رَسُولُ ٱللَّهِ إِلَيْكُمْ ۖ فَلَمَّا زَاغُوٓا۟ أَزَاغَ ٱللَّهُ قُلُوبَهُمْ ۚ وَٱللَّهُ لَا يَهْدِي
ٱلْقَوْمَ ٱلْفَٰسِقِينَ ﴿٥﴾ ﴿الصف﴾

"... And when they turned away, Allah turned their hearts away ..." (61:5)

May He open our hearts to truth and guidance.

---

17. The "illness" mentioned here is explained as doubt, hypocrisy, arrogance and disbelief.

Āyah 11

إِنَّمَا تُنذِرُ مَنِ ٱتَّبَعَ ٱلذِّكْرَ وَخَشِيَ ٱلرَّحْمَٰنَ بِٱلْغَيْبِ ۖ فَبَشِّرْهُ بِمَغْفِرَةٍ وَأَجْرٍ كَرِيمٍ ﴿١١﴾

[11] You can only warn one who follows the Remembrance and fears al-Raḥmān unseen. So give him good tidings of forgiveness and of generous reward.

"The Remembrance" here refers to the Qur'an. It is so named by Allah (ﷻ) to convey to us that its message is not new or unfamiliar. It merely reminds man of that truth already known in the depths of his own soul and witnessed at the beginning of his creation:

وَإِذْ أَخَذَ رَبُّكَ مِنۢ بَنِيٓ ءَادَمَ مِن ظُهُورِهِمْ ذُرِّيَّتَهُمْ وَأَشْهَدَهُمْ عَلَىٰٓ أَنفُسِهِمْ أَلَسْتُ بِرَبِّكُمْ ۖ قَالُوا۟ بَلَىٰ ۛ شَهِدْنَآ ۛ أَن تَقُولُوا۟ يَوْمَ ٱلْقِيَٰمَةِ إِنَّا كُنَّا عَنْ هَٰذَا غَٰفِلِينَ ﴿١٧٢﴾ ﴿الأعراف﴾

"And when your Lord took from the children of Adam—from their loins—their descendants, and made them witness about themselves, (saying), 'Am I not your Lord?' They said, 'Yes, we have witnessed'—so you cannot say on the Day of Judgement, 'Indeed we were unaware of this ...'" (7:172)

Every messenger was appointed by Allah to remind men who had somehow forgotten this truth and turned away from their Lord. And each brought the same message:

لَقَدْ أَرْسَلْنَا نُوحًا إِلَىٰ قَوْمِهِۦ فَقَالَ يَـٰقَوْمِ ٱعْبُدُوا۟ ٱللَّهَ مَا لَكُم مِّنْ إِلَـٰهٍ غَيْرُهُۥٓ إِنِّىٓ أَخَافُ عَلَيْكُمْ عَذَابَ يَوْمٍ عَظِيمٍ ﴿٥٩﴾ ﴿الأعراف﴾

"… He said: O my people, worship Allah. You have no other god but Him …"[18]

Prophethood ended with Muḥammad (ﷺ), and the final Reminder to man remains until the Day of Judgement. It is complete and unaltered as promised by Allah so that there will be no excuse for deviation and so that there will always be men who will follow the true religion:

إِنَّا نَحْنُ نَزَّلْنَا ٱلذِّكْرَ وَإِنَّا لَهُۥ لَحَـٰفِظُونَ ﴿٩﴾ ﴿الحجر﴾

"Verily We have sent down the Remembrance, and verily We are its guardian." (15:9)

But the warning will be of no benefit to those who refuse it. In this *āyah* of Yā Sīn the Prophet (ﷺ) is told by Allah that only a certain kind of person is receptive to the warning. First, one who follows the Qur'an, *ie.,* believes in it, learns it and practices it. The Prophet's companions (ﷺ) used to eagerly await each and every revelation, and once it was heard and understood, they would hasten to apply it to every aspect of their lives. And second, one who fears al-Raḥmān (Allah, the Most Merciful)[19] although he does not

18. See *āyahs* 7:59, 65, 73, 85; 11:50, 61, 84 and 23:23.
19. Allah says:

قُلِ ٱدْعُوا۟ ٱللَّهَ أَوِ ٱدْعُوا۟ ٱلرَّحْمَـٰنَ ۖ أَيًّا مَّا تَدْعُوا۟ فَلَهُ ٱلْأَسْمَآءُ ٱلْحُسْنَىٰ ۚ وَلَا تَجْهَرْ بِصَلَاتِكَ وَلَا تُخَافِتْ بِهَا وَٱبْتَغِ بَيْنَ ذَٰلِكَ سَبِيلًا ﴿١١٠﴾ ﴿الإسراء﴾

"Call upon Allah or call upon al-Raḥmān. Whichever (name) you call, His are the best names." (17:110)

see Him. The Prophet (ﷺ) described *iḥsān* (proficiency in religion) as "worshipping Allah as though you see Him, for even though you do not see Him, indeed He sees you".[20] Allah confirms in another *āyah*:

إِنَّ ٱلَّذِينَ يَخْشَوْنَ رَبَّهُم بِٱلْغَيْبِ لَهُم مَّغْفِرَةٌ وَأَجْرٌ كَبِيرٌ ﴿١٢﴾ ﴿المُلْك﴾

"Those who fear their Lord in the unseen will have forgiveness and great reward." (67:12)

To such people is the Qur'an directed—the believers "who, when Allah is mentioned, their hearts are fearful; and when His verses are recited to them, their faith is increased; and upon their Lord (alone) they depend."[21]

These are the ones deserving good tidings and reassurance that all of their efforts and sacrifices in obedience to Allah will be fully appreciated and generously rewarded by Him.

Āyah 12

إِنَّا نَحْنُ نُحْيِ ٱلْمَوْتَىٰ وَنَكْتُبُ مَا قَدَّمُواْ وَءَاثَٰرَهُمْ ۚ وَكُلَّ شَيْءٍ أَحْصَيْنَٰهُ فِيٓ إِمَامٍ مُّبِينٍ ﴿١٢﴾

[12] It is We who bring the dead to life and record what they have put forth and left behind, and all things We have enumerated in a clear register.

---

20. Muslim.
21. Sūrah al-Anfāl, (8:2)

إِنَّمَا ٱلْمُؤْمِنُونَ ٱلَّذِينَ إِذَا ذُكِرَ ٱللَّهُ وَجِلَتْ قُلُوبُهُمْ وَإِذَا تُلِيَتْ عَلَيْهِمْ ءَايَٰتُهُۥ زَادَتْهُمْ إِيمَٰنًا وَعَلَىٰ رَبِّهِمْ يَتَوَكَّلُونَ ﴿٢﴾ ﴿الأنفال﴾

Ibn Kathīr has asserted that although the obvious meaning in this *āyah* is that Allah will resurrect the dead on the Day of Judgement, it also contains a suggestion that He gives life to such hearts as He wills among the non-believers in the form of guidance and enlightenment after they were once "dead", *ie.,* in a state of unawareness and error. He has supported this view by citing *āyahs* 16 and 17 of Sūrah al-Ḥadīd, in which are mentioned those whose hearts had become hardened, followed by the words: "Know that Allah gives life to the earth after its death. We have made evident to you the signs that perhaps you may understand."[22] Indeed, it is well known that such outstanding men as 'Umar bin al-Khaṭṭāb and Khālid bin al-Walīd were initially enemies of Islam whose hearts were later awakened by Allah.

The word *mawtā* (plural of *mayyit*), previously discussed in relation to a specific *ḥadīth,* unquestionably refers in this *āyah* to "the dead", *ie.,* the lifeless. In other Qur'anic verses similar in meaning to *āyahs* 10 and 11 of this Sūrah, Allah tells His Prophet (ﷺ):

إِنَّكَ لَا تُسْمِعُ ٱلْمَوْتَىٰ وَلَا تُسْمِعُ ٱلصُّمَّ ٱلدُّعَآءَ إِذَا وَلَّوْا۟ مُدْبِرِينَ ﴿٨٠﴾ ﴿النمل﴾

"You cannot make the dead hear,..." (27:80) meaning the dead of heart.

---

22. Sūrah al-Ḥadīd, (57:17)

ٱعْلَمُوٓا۟ أَنَّ ٱللَّهَ يُحْىِ ٱلْأَرْضَ بَعْدَ مَوْتِهَا ۚ قَدْ بَيَّنَّا لَكُمُ ٱلْـَٔايَـٰتِ لَعَلَّكُمْ تَعْقِلُونَ ﴿١٧﴾ ﴿الحديد﴾

It is a certainty that Allah (ﷻ) will bring the dead to life once again for the Judgement. Those who are skeptical of this fact will have their reply, but not here. It will be postponed until the final *āyahs* of the Sūrah after ample evidence has been provided. As for the basis of the Judgement, it is clearly stated in no uncertain terms. It will include all that one has put forth, *ie.,* the deeds that he has sent ahead of him to the Hereafter, either knowingly or unknowingly. And it will also include all that he did upon the earth.

The word *āthār* (plural of *athar)* means "traces", "effects" or "what is left behind". Thus one might say or do something (either good or evil), the effects of which will remain in the physical world or in the hearts of others for some time, perhaps even long after the person's demise. These after effects will be a part of every servant's account.

The Prophet (ﷺ) explained another aspect of *āthār* when he said, "Whoever establishes a good practice (*sunnah*) in Islam will have its reward and the reward of all of those who act according to it after him without lessening their rewards at all. And whoever establishes a bad practice in Islam will carry its sin and the sin of all of those who act according to it after him without lessening their sin at all."[23] And he also stated, "When a son of Adam (*ie.,* man) dies, his deeds are ended except for three: (his) knowledge from which there is benefit, a

23. Muslim.

righteous child who supplicates for him, or a charity which continues on after him."[24]

Additionally, another more specific meaning also given by commentators is "footprints" or "the traces of one's footsteps", citing as an example the Prophet's advice against moving homes closer to the *masjid* since the additional steps from a distance are recorded and the person rewarded for them.

Finally, in this *āyah* Allah (ﷻ) informs us that He keeps track of all things in a clear register (*imām*)—the Book of Deeds. And the record will be complete and accurate:

وَوُضِعَ ٱلْكِتَٰبُ فَتَرَى ٱلْمُجْرِمِينَ مُشْفِقِينَ مِمَّا فِيهِ وَيَقُولُونَ يَٰوَيْلَتَنَا مَالِ هَٰذَا ٱلْكِتَٰبِ لَا يُغَادِرُ صَغِيرَةً وَلَا كَبِيرَةً إِلَّآ أَحْصَىٰهَا ۚ وَوَجَدُوا۟ مَا عَمِلُوا۟ حَاضِرًا ۗ وَلَا يَظْلِمُ رَبُّكَ أَحَدًا ﴿٤٩﴾ ﴿الكهف﴾

"… It does not leave anything small or great except that it has enumerated it …" (18:49)

Our familiarity in recent years with man-made devices that can record, store and later impart information to the eye and ear about many human activities and conditions must certainly facilitate understanding of this concept, although it has always been an essential part of Islamic belief. Man's ability to bring back memories of past events, complete with accompanying emotions, or the playback in a dream of something long forgotten is adequate evidence that what is

---

24. Muslim.

past is not over and dead but continues to exist, is stored, and can be recalled whenever the Creator should will:

هَٰذَا كِتَٰبُنَا يَنطِقُ عَلَيْكُم بِٱلْحَقِّ ۚ إِنَّا كُنَّا نَسْتَنسِخُ مَا كُنتُمْ تَعْمَلُونَ ﴿٢٩﴾ ﴿الجاثية﴾

"This, Our Book (of Deeds), speaks about you in truth. Verily, We were recording what you used to do." (45:29)

ĀYAHS 13–32

وَٱضْرِبْ لَهُم مَّثَلًا أَصْحَـٰبَ ٱلْقَرْيَةِ إِذْ جَآءَهَا ٱلْمُرْسَلُونَ ﴿١٣﴾ إِذْ
أَرْسَلْنَآ إِلَيْهِمُ ٱثْنَيْنِ فَكَذَّبُوهُمَا فَعَزَّزْنَا بِثَالِثٍ فَقَالُوٓا۟ إِنَّآ إِلَيْكُم
مُّرْسَلُونَ ﴿١٤﴾ قَالُوا۟ مَآ أَنتُمْ إِلَّا بَشَرٌ مِّثْلُنَا وَمَآ أَنزَلَ ٱلرَّحْمَـٰنُ مِن
شَىْءٍ إِنْ أَنتُمْ إِلَّا تَكْذِبُونَ ﴿١٥﴾ قَالُوا۟ رَبُّنَا يَعْلَمُ إِنَّآ إِلَيْكُمْ
لَمُرْسَلُونَ ﴿١٦﴾ وَمَا عَلَيْنَآ إِلَّا ٱلْبَلَـٰغُ ٱلْمُبِينُ ﴿١٧﴾ قَالُوٓا۟ إِنَّا تَطَيَّرْنَا
بِكُمْ ۖ لَئِن لَّمْ تَنتَهُوا۟ لَنَرْجُمَنَّكُمْ وَلَيَمَسَّنَّكُم مِّنَّا عَذَابٌ أَلِيمٌ ﴿١٨﴾
قَالُوا۟ طَـٰٓئِرُكُم مَّعَكُمْ ۚ أَئِن ذُكِّرْتُم ۚ بَلْ أَنتُمْ قَوْمٌ مُّسْرِفُونَ ﴿١٩﴾
وَجَآءَ مِنْ أَقْصَا ٱلْمَدِينَةِ رَجُلٌ يَسْعَىٰ قَالَ يَـٰقَوْمِ ٱتَّبِعُوا۟
ٱلْمُرْسَلِينَ ﴿٢٠﴾ ٱتَّبِعُوا۟ مَن لَّا يَسْـَٔلُكُمْ أَجْرًا وَهُم مُّهْتَدُونَ ﴿٢١﴾
وَمَا لِىَ لَآ أَعْبُدُ ٱلَّذِى فَطَرَنِى وَإِلَيْهِ تُرْجَعُونَ ﴿٢٢﴾ ءَأَتَّخِذُ مِن
دُونِهِۦٓ ءَالِهَةً إِن يُرِدْنِ ٱلرَّحْمَـٰنُ بِضُرٍّ لَّا تُغْنِ عَنِّى شَفَـٰعَتُهُمْ شَيْـًٔا
وَلَا يُنقِذُونِ ﴿٢٣﴾ إِنِّىٓ إِذًا لَّفِى ضَلَـٰلٍ مُّبِينٍ ﴿٢٤﴾ إِنِّىٓ ءَامَنتُ بِرَبِّكُمْ
فَٱسْمَعُونِ ﴿٢٥﴾ قِيلَ ٱدْخُلِ ٱلْجَنَّةَ ۖ قَالَ يَـٰلَيْتَ قَوْمِى يَعْلَمُونَ ﴿٢٦﴾
بِمَا غَفَرَ لِى رَبِّى وَجَعَلَنِى مِنَ ٱلْمُكْرَمِينَ ﴿٢٧﴾ وَمَآ أَنزَلْنَا عَلَىٰ

قَوۡمِهِۦ مِنۢ بَعۡدِهِۦ مِن جُندٖ مِّنَ ٱلسَّمَآءِ وَمَا كُنَّا مُنزِلِينَ ٢٨
إِن كَانَتۡ إِلَّا صَيۡحَةٗ وَٰحِدَةٗ فَإِذَا هُمۡ خَٰمِدُونَ ٢٩ يَٰحَسۡرَةً عَلَى
ٱلۡعِبَادِۚ مَا يَأۡتِيهِم مِّن رَّسُولٍ إِلَّا كَانُواْ بِهِۦ يَسۡتَهۡزِءُونَ ٣٠ أَلَمۡ
يَرَوۡاْ كَمۡ أَهۡلَكۡنَا قَبۡلَهُم مِّنَ ٱلۡقُرُونِ أَنَّهُمۡ إِلَيۡهِمۡ لَا يَرۡجِعُونَ ٣١
وَإِن كُلّٞ لَّمَّا جَمِيعٞ لَّدَيۡنَا مُحۡضَرُونَ ٣٢

[13] And put before them an example—the people of the city when the messengers came to it—[14] When We sent them two, but they denied them; so We strengthened them with a third, and they said, "Indeed we are messengers to you." [15] They said, "You are none but human beings like ourselves, and al-Raḥmān has revealed nothing. You are only lying." [16] They said, "Our Lord knows that we are messengers to you. [17] And we are not responsible except for clear notification." [18] They said, "We consider you a bad omen. If you do not desist, we will stone you and you will be touched by a painful punishment from us." [19] They said, "Your omen is with yourselves. Is it because you were reminded? No, you are but a transgressing people." [20] And there came from the farthest end of the city a man, running. He said, "O my people, follow the messengers. [21] Follow those who do not ask of you any payment and are (rightly) guided. [22] And why should I not worship the One Who created me and to Whom you shall return? [23] Should I take (for myself) deities other than Him, when al-Raḥmān means for me some adversity their intercession

will not avail me at all, nor can they save me? [24] I would then certainly be in manifest error. [25] Verily, I have believed in your Lord, so listen to me." [26] It was said, "Enter Paradise." He said, "I wish my people could know [27] of how my Lord has forgiven me and made me among the honored." [28] And We did not send down upon his people after him any soldiers from Heaven, nor would We have done so. [29] It was not but a single blast and they were (immediately) extinguished. [30] Alas for the servants. No messenger comes to them except that they ridicule him. [31] Do they not see how many generations We have destroyed before them—that they will not return to them? [32] But all of them will yet be brought into Our presence.

The Effect of Stories in the Qur'an

Being the words of Allah (ﷻ), Qur'anic narrations contain pure, historical truths free from the fantasy and imaginings found in the works of human authors. Allah confirms:

وَٱلَّذِىٓ أَوۡحَيۡنَآ إِلَيۡكَ مِنَ ٱلۡكِتَٰبِ هُوَ ٱلۡحَقُّ مُصَدِّقٗا لِّمَا بَيۡنَ
يَدَيۡهِۗ إِنَّ ٱللَّهَ بِعِبَادِهِۦ لَخَبِيرُۢ بَصِيرٞ ٣١ ﴿فَاطِر﴾

"And that which We have inspired to you of the Scripture is the truth …" (35:31)

The Qur'an makes use of the story's natural attraction to impart certain lessons and implant them in the mind of the reader or listener.

There are three types of stories related in the Qur'an:

1. Those about prophets
2. Those about ancient peoples or events
3. Those about events which occurred during the time of Prophet Muḥammad (ﷺ)

Sūrah Yā Sīn contains a unique account belonging to the second category, in which the result of rejection and rebellion is exposed as well as that of faith and *jihād.*

Āyah 13

وَٱضْرِبْ لَهُم مَّثَلًا أَصْحَٰبَ ٱلْقَرْيَةِ إِذْ جَآءَهَا ٱلْمُرْسَلُونَ ۝١٣

[13] And put before them an example—the people of the city when the messengers came to it.

"And put before them an example ..." Allah (ﷻ) orders Prophet Muḥammad (ﷺ) to give this illustration from the past which has been revealed to him. The Qur'anic style brings the scene before its audience almost as though they are eyewitnesses.

"... The people of the city when the messengers came to it ..." Although some early commentators relying upon Christian sources have held that this city was Antioch and that the messengers were sent by Prophet 'Īsā (عليه السلام), there is no support for this view in the Qur'an or in any authentic *ḥadīth.* On the contrary, in refuting it, Ibn Kathīr has cited well-known historical facts as counter-evidence.[1] Since the objective behind Qur'anic stories is

1. In any case, as mentioned on page xii, Christian and Jewish sources cannot be considered valid unless confirmed in the Qur'an or in *ḥadīths*.

to remind, warn and advise, the naming of specific places would normally not serve any useful purpose. Allah (ﷻ) does not distract from the narration of this story with unnecessary details but goes directly on to the point of the lesson.

Āyah 14

إِذْ أَرْسَلْنَآ إِلَيْهِمُ ٱثْنَيْنِ فَكَذَّبُوهُمَا فَعَزَّزْنَا بِثَالِثٍ فَقَالُوٓا۟
إِنَّآ إِلَيْكُم مُّرْسَلُونَ ﴿١٤﴾

> [14] When We sent them two, but they denied them; so We strengthened them with a third and they said, "Indeed we are messengers to you."

Here is a settlement to which Allah had sent two messengers. Before the Final Scripture was revealed to Prophet Muḥammad (ﷺ), messengers were sent to peoples who had forgotten their Creator (worshipping and obeying others besides Him) and had strayed into evil and corruption. One can only speculate as to why a single messenger was not sufficient for this particular community. Nevertheless, we are informed that since two were denied, Allah saw fit to reinforce them with a third. The messengers immediately and publicly announce themselves, for their message (and that of all prophets and of the propagators after them) is a clear and direct one without mystery or deception: "Indeed we are messengers to you."

Āyah 15

قَالُواْ مَآ أَنتُمۡ إِلَّا بَشَرٌ مِّثۡلُنَا وَمَآ أَنزَلَ ٱلرَّحۡمَٰنُ مِن شَيۡءٍ إِنۡ أَنتُمۡ إِلَّا تَكۡذِبُونَ ﴿١٥﴾

[15] They said, "You are none but human beings like ourselves, and al-Raḥmān has revealed nothing. You are only lying."

These three statements put forward by the obstinate people reflect and summarize the position of those who reject the divine message in every generation. If they had been open to guidance, the disbelievers of Quraysh would surely have seen their own attitudes reflected in this dialogue. When following the story through to its conclusion, they would have found adequate warning about the danger of similar behavior towards any messenger sent by Allah—in particular the one who was then among them.

The three arguments alleged by the rejecters are as follows:

1. "You are none but human beings like ourselves."

The disbelievers suppose that any messenger coming from Allah should be an angel or a supernatural being. Allah states:

وَمَا مَنَعَ ٱلنَّاسَ أَن يُؤۡمِنُوٓاْ إِذۡ جَآءَهُمُ ٱلۡهُدَىٰٓ إِلَّآ أَن قَالُوٓاْ أَبَعَثَ ٱللَّهُ بَشَرٗا رَّسُولٗا ﴿٩٤﴾ ﴿الإسراء﴾

"And what prevented the people from believing when

guidance came to them except that they said, 'Has Allah sent a human messenger?!'" (17:94)

Prophet Nūḥ (ﷺ) faced the same objection,[2] as did Hūd[3] (ﷺ), Ṣāliḥ[4] (ﷺ) and Muḥammad (ﷺ).[5] "Because they are human beings like ourselves, we cannot accept them as messengers from Allah," declared their opponents.

In their pretense of intelligence and sophistication, the objectors forget a simple fact—that education by demonstration is an essential aspect of the revelation. Any creature other than a man could not reasonably be accepted as a pattern of conduct and behavior. One could easily justify failure to practice a way of life taught by an angel or other type of being. The vast difference between its physical and psychological nature and that of man would be cited as a prohibiting factor. In His wisdom, Allah (ﷻ) willed that certain men (*ie.,* His messengers) should not only expound but also demonstrate the practical application of divine teachings. The fact that those human beings were given the special capacity for reception of messages from the Creator of the universe far beyond the limits of creation is surely no less a miracle than what the skeptics demand, but their minds and hearts are closed to the obvious truth.

The Qur'an states simply that every messenger ever sent to earth by Allah was a human being.[6] It argues:

---

2. See 23:24.
3. See 23:33–34.
4. See 54:24.
5. See 25:7.
6. See 21:7–8 and 25:20.

قُل لَّوْ كَانَ فِي ٱلْأَرْضِ مَلَـٰٓئِكَةٌ يَمْشُونَ مُطْمَئِنِّينَ لَنَزَّلْنَا
عَلَيْهِم مِّنَ ٱلسَّمَآءِ مَلَكًا رَّسُولًا ﴿٩٥﴾ ﴿الإسراء﴾

"Say, 'If there were angels walking securely upon the earth, We would have sent down to them from Heaven an angel as a messenger'" (17:95). Thus, a human messenger is most suitable as an example to the earth's human inhabitants.

2. "Al-Raḥmān has revealed nothing."

Even if they admit the existence of a Creator, as most of the ancients did, their denial that He would continue to care for His creatures and communicate His will to them leads the complacent to reject revelation and prophethood. Sensing that a message from Allah Almighty could not be ignored, they chose to completely avoid confrontation with responsibility by claiming that He never sent down any such message in the first place. In Sūrah al-Mulk the inhabitants of Hellfire confess to this, saying:

قَالُوا۟ بَلَىٰ قَدْ جَآءَنَا نَذِيرٌ فَكَذَّبْنَا وَقُلْنَا مَا نَزَّلَ ٱللَّهُ مِن شَىْءٍ إِنْ
أَنتُمْ إِلَّا فِي ضَلَـٰلٍ كَبِيرٍ ﴿٩﴾ ﴿الملك﴾

"Yes, a warner had come to us, but we denied and said, 'Allah has revealed nothing. You are but in a great delusion.'" (67:9)

3. "You are only lying."

By accusing the messengers of falsehood, the arrogant ones seek to prevent the development of trust in them among the population. They have begun to feel the threat that the truth would bring to their evil establishment. Those intruders must be discredited in order to preserve the status-quo, in short, the community's worldly interests and institutions based upon tyranny and oppression.

Āyahs 16–17

قَالُواْ رَبُّنَا يَعۡلَمُ إِنَّآ إِلَيۡكُمۡ لَمُرۡسَلُونَ ﴿١٦﴾ وَمَا عَلَيۡنَآ إِلَّا
ٱلۡبَلَٰغُ ٱلۡمُبِينُ ﴿١٧﴾

> [16] They said, "Our Lord knows that we are messengers to you." [17] "And we are not responsible except for clear notification."

Confidently, the messengers state that they are aware of the limits of their responsibility. They have conveyed the information entrusted to them by Allah and fulfilled their duty, and after that the people are free to decide for themselves. But a wrong decision made by them in spite of clear warnings cannot be blamed upon the messengers.

Āyah 18

قَالُوٓاْ إِنَّا تَطَيَّرۡنَا بِكُمۡۖ لَئِن لَّمۡ تَنتَهُواْ لَنَرۡجُمَنَّكُمۡ وَلَيَمَسَّنَّكُم
مِّنَّا عَذَابٌ أَلِيمٞ ﴿١٨﴾

> [18] They said, "We consider you a bad omen. If you do not desist, we will stone you and you will be touched by a painful punishment from us ..."

The evil ones are becoming increasingly anxious. They call upon the ignorant and superstitious nature of the population, hoping to attach a stigma to the three messengers by suggesting that they will be a cause of ill fortune[7] and, therefore, should be eliminated. The call to righteousness and to the worship of Allah must be aborted if their own social system is to survive. The oppressors will not tolerate reformers among them. If they cannot discredit them or discourage them with harsh words, then stronger measures will be taken.

Thus, as it does in every age, tyranny exposes its own failure. It cannot withstand the expression of truth or even of the least bit of criticism. Opposition must be silenced. Power and authority in the land must be retained at all costs. The people must not think of change; they must not hear of it. They must not know that it is possible. They must believe that in their present situation all is well, or at least that nothing is better. They must be protected from alien influence, from insurgents who question corrupt authority, undermine security and sow discontentment.

Tyranny cannot allow the outspoken bearers of truth to go unchecked. It is helpless against reason and cannot hope to persuade; it can only strike out violently in frustration and anger. Any threat of such action should be taken very seriously indeed. The messengers are warned: Either cease your *da'wah* efforts or expect the worst!

---

7. The word *taṭayyarnā* is derived from *ṭāra* (طَارَ), meaning "flew". Among the ancient superstitions was the one that a bird be released if an important decision was to be made. If it flew to the left, it was seen as a bad omen.

Āyah 19

قَالُوا۟ طَـٰٓئِرُكُم مَّعَكُمْ ۚ أَئِن ذُكِّرْتُم ۚ بَلْ أَنتُمْ قَوْمٌ
مُّسْرِفُونَ ﴿١٩﴾

> [19] They said, "Your omen is with yourselves. Is it because you were reminded? No, you are but a transgressing people."

The response of the messengers is again a simple truth. Superstition is a pastime of the ignorant, who are unable to relate events to their proper causes, who refuse to admit failures, and who claim that any ill which befalls them is due to an evil spirit or some unaccountable foreign influence. Often they seek to blame others for agitating that mysterious force against them. But, in reality, one's fate is in his own hands in as much as the decision is his, whether to follow the guidance imparted by Allah and reap its benefit or to reject it and bear the consequences. The people are told: Any evil that should befall you, after this information has reached you, is merely the result of your own misdeeds and bad intentions.

And pointing directly to the example before them, the messengers put the question: "Is it because you were reminded?" Do you reward those who care for your own best interests, reminding you of all that is good and warning you against that which is harmful, with defiance, slander and threat? For our exertion on your behalf you would stone us and torture us? "No, you are but a transgressing people," exceeding all limits of justice and decency.

Āyah 20

وَجَآءَ مِنْ أَقْصَا ٱلْمَدِينَةِ رَجُلٌ يَسْعَىٰ قَالَ يَـٰقَوْمِ ٱتَّبِعُوا۟
ٱلْمُرْسَلِينَ ﴿٢٠﴾

[20] And there came from the farthest end of the city a man, running. He said, "O my people, follow the messengers."

It is possible, as some commentators have suggested, that at this point the defiant community was about to kill the three messengers. In contrast to their violent reaction against the truth is this example of a true believer who exerts himself in its defense.

A lone man driven by sense of duty propels himself towards the gathering in the center of town. He has heard the message and understood it. Its appeal to reason has opened his eyes. Its evidence is such as to leave no doubt. Certain that the warnings are true and concerned for his people's welfare, he cannot remain silent. Not wasting a moment with introductions or pleasantries, he comes straight to the point: "O my people, follow the messengers."

Āyah 21

ٱتَّبِعُوا۟ مَن لَّا يَسْـَٔلُكُمْ أَجْرًا وَهُم مُّهْتَدُونَ ﴿٢١﴾

[21] Follow those who do not ask of you any payment and are (rightly) guided.

The believer points out that the messengers are not seeking any worldly gain for all of their trouble. This is surely proof of sincerity and truthfulness, for who would undertake such a thankless task otherwise? Who would oppose familiar traditions to which the people are attached and will defend blindly? Who would expose himself to ridicule and insult, bearing the anger and assault of the disbelievers with no compensation in this world … unless he expected a greater reward from another source? All prophets sent by Allah to mankind have clarified their position to the people, saying:

وَمَآ أَسۡـَٔلُكُمۡ عَلَيۡهِ مِنۡ أَجۡرٍۖ إِنۡ أَجۡرِيَ إِلَّا عَلَىٰ رَبِّ ٱلۡعَٰلَمِينَ ﴿١٠٩﴾ ﴿الشعراء﴾

"And I do not ask of you any payment for it. My payment is only from the Lord of the Worlds." (26:109)[8]

The fact that they are rightly guided is plain from the nature of their message, for they invite only to the worship of one God, Who is the Creator of mankind and of all things. Their creed is clear and simple, free of mystery, secrecy or superstition. Compatible with *fiṭrah*[9] and with human nature, it satisfies both the heart and the intellect. And there is adequate evidence to support it, whether in the visible universe or within the human person himself:

سَنُرِيهِمۡ ءَايَٰتِنَا فِي ٱلۡأٓفَاقِ وَفِيٓ أَنفُسِهِمۡ حَتَّىٰ يَتَبَيَّنَ لَهُمۡ أَنَّهُ ٱلۡحَقُّۗ
أَوَلَمۡ يَكۡفِ بِرَبِّكَ أَنَّهُۥ عَلَىٰ كُلِّ شَيۡءٖ شَهِيدٌ ﴿٥٣﴾ ﴿فصلت﴾

8. See also 26: 127, 145, 164, and 180.

9. The natural inclination of man to worship his Creator before his corruption by external influences. The Prophet (ﷺ) said, "Every child is born with *fiṭrah*. Then his parents make him a Jew, a Christian or a Majūsī." (Al-Bukhārī and Muslim.)

"We shall show them Our signs in the horizons and within themselves until it becomes evident to them that it is the truth …" (41:53)

Āyah 22

وَمَا لِىَ لَآ أَعۡبُدُ ٱلَّذِى فَطَرَنِى وَإِلَيۡهِ تُرۡجَعُونَ ﴿٢٢﴾

[22] "And why should I not worship the One Who created me and to Whom you shall return?"

The believer appeals to his people's reason and common sense. Using himself as an example to illustrate his point, he responds to their implied question: What! Should we abandon what our fathers worshipped for the worship of Allah alone? He answers with questions of his own: Does it stand to reason that while Allah has created me, sustains me and controls my destiny I should worship other than Him? Would I not then be ungrateful and undeserving of His favor? And since you, as well as I, will ultimately return to our Creator, would it not be foolish on our part to avoid establishing a good relationship with Him?

Prophet Muḥammad (ﷺ) was directed by Allah to use a similar argument and say:

قُلۡ يَـٰٓأَيُّهَا ٱلنَّاسُ إِن كُنتُمۡ فِى شَكٍّ مِّن دِينِى فَلَآ أَعۡبُدُ ٱلَّذِينَ تَعۡبُدُونَ مِن دُونِ ٱللَّهِ وَلَـٰكِنۡ أَعۡبُدُ ٱللَّهَ ٱلَّذِى يَتَوَفَّىٰكُمۡ ۖ وَأُمِرۡتُ أَنۡ أَكُونَ مِنَ ٱلۡمُؤۡمِنِينَ ﴿١٠٤﴾ ﴿يونس﴾

"… I do not worship those whom you worship other than Allah, but I worship Allah, Who takes your souls …" (10:104)

Āyah 23

ءَأَتَّخِذُ مِن دُونِهِۦٓ ءَالِهَةً إِن يُرِدۡنِ ٱلرَّحۡمَٰنُ بِضُرّٖ لَّا تُغۡنِ
عَنِّي شَفَٰعَتُهُمۡ شَيۡـٔٗا وَلَا يُنقِذُونِ ٢٣

[23] "Should I take (for myself) deities other than Him, when al-Raḥmān means for me some adversity their intercession will not avail me at all, nor can they save me?"

Going on to expose the error in a position which opposes the natural, instinctive and reasonable object of worship, the believer states that no power can prevent what Allah, al-Raḥmān, has willed. "So," he asks, "why waste one's time and effort on false and impotent gods?"

Taking a deity for oneself involves the question of authority, since the basis of worship is obedience. Who should have the right to govern man if not the One Who created him and knows him better than he knows himself? But man, in his ignorance and injustice, readily gives his loyalty to other "authorities"—to humans like himself, customs, traditions, political ideologies, fashionable trends, material possessions and physical passions—raising them by his devotion to the status of gods, enslaving himself to serve them, and ultimately degrading his own humanity. Yet none of these can save one from misfortune, if willed by Allah (ﷻ):

وَإِن يَمْسَسْكَ ٱللَّهُ بِضُرٍّ فَلَا كَاشِفَ لَهُۥٓ إِلَّا هُوَ ۖ وَإِن يَمْسَسْكَ بِخَيْرٍ فَهُوَ عَلَىٰ كُلِّ شَىْءٍ قَدِيرٌ ﴿١٧﴾ ﴿الأنعام﴾

"If Allah touches you with adversity, no one can remove it except Him …" (6:17)

Allah is completely superior to and unlike anything He has created. He alone is the cause of all that takes place in creation—the original source of all things and all occurrences—totally dependent upon Allah for his continued existence on earth and then for His mercy in the Hereafter. Man is in no logical position to invite His anger.

To the claim of those who say they merely worship others as intermediaries, the believer adds that the intercession of false gods is useless. Allah confirms:

أَمِ ٱتَّخَذُوا۟ مِن دُونِ ٱللَّهِ شُفَعَآءَ ۚ قُلْ أَوَلَوْ كَانُوا۟ لَا يَمْلِكُونَ شَيْـًٔا وَلَا يَعْقِلُونَ ﴿٤٣﴾ قُل لِّلَّهِ ٱلشَّفَـٰعَةُ جَمِيعًا ۖ لَّهُۥ مُلْكُ ٱلسَّمَـٰوَٰتِ وَٱلْأَرْضِ ۖ ثُمَّ إِلَيْهِ تُرْجَعُونَ ﴿٤٤﴾ ﴿الزمر﴾

"Or do they take as intercessors other than Allah? Say, 'Even though they cannot control anything nor can they reason?!' Say, 'To Allah belongs (the right to allow) intercession entirely. To Him belongs the dominion of the heavens and the earth. Then (finally) to Him you will be returned.'" (39:43–44)

And He says: "Who is it that can intercede with Him except by His permission?" (2:255)

Āyahs 24–25

إِنِّيٓ إِذٗا لَّفِي ضَلَٰلٖ مُّبِينٍ ﴿٢٤﴾ إِنِّيٓ ءَامَنتُ بِرَبِّكُمۡ
فَٱسۡمَعُونِ ﴿٢٥﴾

[24] "I would then certainly be in manifest error." [25] "Verily, I have believed in your Lord, so listen to me."

After putting forth his case based upon reason, the believing man concludes his argument: How could I accept deities other than al-Raḥmān, Allah, Most Merciful, when He is the only one worthy of my worship and obedience? It is obvious that I, as well as anyone who should prefer an inferior alternative, would be making a grave misjudgement. Then he confirms that he has taken the only course open to an intelligent person, urging his people to do the same.

Thus speaks the believer, standing courageously before the crowd, knowing that whatever the outcome, Allah is with him, hearing and seeing, witnessing his efforts and his testimony. Surely his reward cannot be far away.

Āyahs 26–27

قِيلَ ٱدۡخُلِ ٱلۡجَنَّةَۖ قَالَ يَٰلَيۡتَ قَوۡمِي يَعۡلَمُونَ ﴿٢٦﴾ بِمَا
غَفَرَ لِي رَبِّي وَجَعَلَنِي مِنَ ٱلۡمُكۡرَمِينَ ﴿٢٧﴾

[26] It was said, "Enter Paradise." He said, "I wish my people could know [27] of how my Lord has forgiven me and made me among the honored."

Martyrdom is not obtained easily. Such men as this believer are chosen by Allah for the honor after having proven their worthiness.

The abrupt transfer in scene from that earthly confrontation to the Hereafter conveys the meaning that the believer's death was immediate, and at the hands of those he had tried to guide. Ibn Kathīr has related, "When he said that (*ie.,* "Verily, I have believed in your Lord, so listen to me."), they leaped upon him with one leap and killed him, and there was no one to defend him." Ibn Mas'ūd mentioned that they trampled him under their feet. And Qutādah said, "They began throwing stones at him while he kept saying, 'O Allah, guide my people, for they know not,' until they slew him—may Allah have mercy upon him."

However the tragedy occurred, the ugly and violent death suggested here, along with previous background information, serves to portray the depths of depravity to which man is capable of sinking when he disassociates himself from divine guidance and consciousness of Allah. How often have similar scenes taken place in the past and present, in public and private—the hysterical frenzy of human beasts who cannot bear truth and justice. Angry, contorted faces thirst for blood, consumed with hatred for those whose only crime is that they accept the authority of Allah above all else. When Fir'awn disclosed his intention to kill Prophet Mūsā (عليه السلام), another believing man stood up in his defense with a word of truth:

وَقَالَ رَجُلٌ مُّؤْمِنٌ مِّنْ ءَالِ فِرْعَوْنَ يَكْتُمُ إِيمَـٰنَهُۥٓ أَتَقْتُلُونَ رَجُلًا أَن يَقُولَ رَبِّىَ ٱللَّهُ وَقَدْ جَآءَكُم بِٱلْبَيِّنَـٰتِ مِن رَّبِّكُمْ ۖ وَإِن يَكُ كَـٰذِبًا فَعَلَيْهِ كَذِبُهُۥ ۖ وَإِن يَكُ صَادِقًا يُصِبْكُم بَعْضُ ٱلَّذِى يَعِدُكُمْ ۖ إِنَّ ٱللَّهَ لَا يَهْدِى مَنْ هُوَ مُسْرِفٌ كَذَّابٌ ﴿٢٨﴾ ﴿غَافِر﴾

"... Do you kill a man (only) because he says, 'My Lord is Allah' and has brought you evidences from your Lord?..." (40:28)

Al-Bukhārī related that when one of the idol-worshippers attacked the Prophet (ﷺ) near the Ka'bah, trying to strangle him with the Prophet's own clothing, Abū Bakr rushed in to prevent him, weeping and shouting out the aforementioned *āyah* from beginning to end.

Submission to the will of Allah, the Exalted, by any sector of society has always been a problem for the ignorant majority and is viewed by them as a danger. Clearly, truth and falsehood are incompatible and cannot tolerate each other.

About those who drove men, women, and children into trenches of fire for refusing to renounce their religion, Allah (ﷻ) said:

وَمَا نَقَمُوا۟ مِنْهُمْ إِلَّآ أَن يُؤْمِنُوا۟ بِٱللَّهِ ٱلْعَزِيزِ ٱلْحَمِيدِ ﴿٨﴾ ﴿البُرُوج﴾

"And they took not revenge against them except (for) that they believed in Allah, the Almighty, the Praiseworthy." (85:8)

Any individual or community whose lord is Allah will never accept a human substitute or an inferior ideal. Here the threat to traditional, materialistic culture becomes evident.

The enemies of Allah are helpless against Him. They can only vent their frustrations against His sincere servants, but in doing so they merely hasten and increase His reward to them.

Thus, the believing man's death sustained for the cause of Allah has made Paradise due to him. He is told without delay, "Enter Paradise." His murder at the hands of the hostile oppressors is the vehicle which carries him from the world of trial, hardship and fear to that of peace, security and honor.

Despite his painful experience, the martyred believer bears no ill feeling toward his murderers. He is not their enemy but simply the enemy of their transgressions. If only they could be made aware of the countless blessings and rewards awaiting the faithful so that they could change their ways. "I wish my people could know", he says.

The Qur'an has given a glimpse into the Hereafter to reassure us that in spite of his apparent defeat at the hands of the aggressors, the believer's struggle to uphold truth was not in vain. For there he is, enjoying rewards far beyond what he had earned through the mercy of Allah—and sufficient to be mentioned at this time is the forgiveness and honor which has been bestowed upon him.

In Ibn Isḥāq's *sīrah* it is related that Musaylimah the Liar[10] interrogated Ḥabīb bin Zayd concerning the Prophet (ﷺ) and then said to him, "Do you testify that he is the messenger of Allah?" "Yes," replied Ḥabīb. He said, "Do you testify that I am the messenger of Allah?" "I do not hear," was the reply. So Musaylimah (may the curse of Allah be upon him) said, "So, you hear that (question) but do not hear this one?!" "Yes," he replied. Thereupon he had his limbs cut off, joint by joint, repeating the question each time. But he gained nothing by it ... until finally his victim expired. Upon hearing that the martyr's name was Ḥabīb, Ka'b al-Aḥbār said, "And by Allah, the name of the man in Yā Sīn was Ḥabīb." But Allah knows best.[11]

Āyahs 28–29

وَمَآ أَنزَلْنَا عَلَىٰ قَوْمِهِۦ مِنۢ بَعْدِهِۦ مِن جُندٍ مِّنَ ٱلسَّمَآءِ وَمَا كُنَّا مُنزِلِينَ ﴿٢٨﴾ إِن كَانَتْ إِلَّا صَيْحَةً وَٰحِدَةً فَإِذَا هُمْ خَٰمِدُونَ ﴿٢٩﴾

[28] And We did not send down upon his people after him any soldiers from Heaven, nor would We have done so. [29] It was not but a single blast and they were (immediately) extinguished.

The believer had met the result of his efforts—the eternal

10. Musaylimah al-Kadhdhāb (the Liar) was an impostor who claimed prophethood during the lifetime of Muḥammad (ﷺ).
11. Quoted from Ibn Kathīr.

reward of Paradise. As for the defiant ones, their fate was sealed by their own evil actions, just as the messengers had foretold. For Allah (ﷻ) did not even consider them worth sending angels to punish them, as had been done with other evil communities. Said Ibn Mas'ūd, "It was much simpler than that." Those who had denied Allah's messengers and killed His faithful servant met with a vengeance swifter than their own.

Commentators have explained that Allah disdained to send His army of angels to deal with such a despicable population. Rather, He brought about their destruction by a mere shout from Jibrīl, causing them to collapse and die at once, just as a raging fire is extinguished, leaving no trace except dead ashes.

Āyah 30

يَـٰحَسْرَةً عَلَى ٱلْعِبَادِ ۚ مَا يَأْتِيهِم مِّن رَّسُولٍ إِلَّا كَانُوا۟ بِهِۦ يَسْتَهْزِءُونَ ﴿٣٠﴾

[30] Alas for the servants. There comes not a messenger to them but they ridicule him.

Ignorant men mock at Allah's prophets, or anyone who takes Religion seriously. But they do not reflect that such levity reacts on themselves. Their own lives are ruined and they cease to count. If they study history, they will see that countless generations were destroyed before them because they did not take Truth seriously and undermined the very basis of their individual and collective existence.

Āyahs 31–32

أَلَمْ يَرَوْا۟ كَمْ أَهْلَكْنَا قَبْلَهُم مِّنَ ٱلْقُرُونِ أَنَّهُمْ إِلَيْهِمْ لَا
يَرْجِعُونَ ﴿٣١﴾ وَإِن كُلٌّ لَّمَّا جَمِيعٌ لَّدَيْنَا مُحْضَرُونَ ﴿٣٢﴾

> [31] Do they not see how many generations We have destroyed before them—that they will not return to them? [32] But all of them will yet be brought into Our presence.

Will they not benefit from previous examples? The question is addressed to any and all who think that they can escape the justice of their Lord—the evil community described in this Sūrah, the Quraysh in their opposition to Prophet Muḥammad (ﷺ), or the tyrants and oppressors of every age, who persecute and pour vengeance upon those who seek to establish Allah's law upon the earth.

Have any of them ever returned to the world to enjoy the fruits of their endeavors? Or have they been taken away forever, seized by the Angel of Death and dragged unwillingly out of this life to face the anger of their Creator, Who says:

نُمَتِّعُهُمْ قَلِيلًا ثُمَّ نَضْطَرُّهُمْ إِلَىٰ عَذَابٍ غَلِيظٍ ﴿٢٤﴾ ﴿لقمان﴾

"We grant them enjoyment for a little; then We shall force them to a massive punishment." (31:24)

The Prophet (ﷺ) said, "Allah, exalted is He, extends the time of the oppressor, but when He seizes him, He will not let him escape." Then he recited:

وَكَذَٰلِكَ أَخْذُ رَبِّكَ إِذَآ أَخَذَ ٱلْقُرَىٰ وَهِىَ ظَٰلِمَةٌ ۚ إِنَّ أَخْذَهُۥٓ أَلِيمٌ
شَدِيدٌ ﴿١٠٢﴾ ﴿هود﴾

"And thus is the seizure of your Lord when He seizes the cities while they are transgressing. Verily His seizure is painful and severe." (11:102)[12]

Every people and every nation from the past, present and future will be brought forward for their account on the Day of Judgement, stripped of all their authority and earthly possessions. "That day Allah will fold up the heavens in His right hand and fold up the earth in His left hand, saying, 'I am the Sovereign. Where are the tyrants? Where are the arrogants?!'"[13]

With this notice the narration is concluded, leaving every heart to reflect upon its lesson.

---

12. Muslim.
13. Portion of a *ḥadīth* related by Muslim.

ĀYAHS 33–44

وَءَايَةٌ لَّهُمُ ٱلْأَرْضُ ٱلْمَيْتَةُ أَحْيَيْنَٰهَا وَأَخْرَجْنَا مِنْهَا حَبًّا فَمِنْهُ
يَأْكُلُونَ ﴿٣٣﴾ وَجَعَلْنَا فِيهَا جَنَّٰتٍ مِّن نَّخِيلٍ وَأَعْنَٰبٍ وَفَجَّرْنَا فِيهَا
مِنَ ٱلْعُيُونِ ﴿٣٤﴾ لِيَأْكُلُوا۟ مِن ثَمَرِهِۦ وَمَا عَمِلَتْهُ أَيْدِيهِمْ ۖ أَفَلَا
يَشْكُرُونَ ﴿٣٥﴾ سُبْحَٰنَ ٱلَّذِى خَلَقَ ٱلْأَزْوَٰجَ كُلَّهَا مِمَّا تُنۢبِتُ
ٱلْأَرْضُ وَمِنْ أَنفُسِهِمْ وَمِمَّا لَا يَعْلَمُونَ ﴿٣٦﴾ وَءَايَةٌ لَّهُمُ ٱلَّيْلُ
نَسْلَخُ مِنْهُ ٱلنَّهَارَ فَإِذَا هُم مُّظْلِمُونَ ﴿٣٧﴾ وَٱلشَّمْسُ تَجْرِى لِمُسْتَقَرٍّ
لَّهَا ۚ ذَٰلِكَ تَقْدِيرُ ٱلْعَزِيزِ ٱلْعَلِيمِ ﴿٣٨﴾ وَٱلْقَمَرَ قَدَّرْنَٰهُ مَنَازِلَ حَتَّىٰ
عَادَ كَٱلْعُرْجُونِ ٱلْقَدِيمِ ﴿٣٩﴾ لَا ٱلشَّمْسُ يَنۢبَغِى لَهَآ أَن تُدْرِكَ
ٱلْقَمَرَ وَلَا ٱلَّيْلُ سَابِقُ ٱلنَّهَارِ ۚ وَكُلٌّ فِى فَلَكٍ يَسْبَحُونَ ﴿٤٠﴾ وَءَايَةٌ
لَّهُمْ أَنَّا حَمَلْنَا ذُرِّيَّتَهُمْ فِى ٱلْفُلْكِ ٱلْمَشْحُونِ ﴿٤١﴾ وَخَلَقْنَا لَهُم مِّن
مِّثْلِهِۦ مَا يَرْكَبُونَ ﴿٤٢﴾ وَإِن نَّشَأْ نُغْرِقْهُمْ فَلَا صَرِيخَ لَهُمْ وَلَا هُمْ
يُنقَذُونَ ﴿٤٣﴾ إِلَّا رَحْمَةً مِّنَّا وَمَتَٰعًا إِلَىٰ حِينٍ ﴿٤٤﴾

[33] And a sign for them is the dead earth. We have brought it to life and brought forth from it seeds from which they then eat. [34] And We made therein

gardens of date-palms and grapes and caused springs to burst forth therefrom [35] So that they may eat of its fruit. And their bands have not produced it, so will they not give thanks? [36] Praise be to Him Who created all pairs—from what the earth grows and from themselves and from that which they do not know. [37] And a sign for them is the night. We strip from it the day, so they are left in darkness. [38] And the sun runs on course towards its final destination. That is the calculation of the Almighty the All-Knowing. [39] And the moon—We have determined for it phases until it returns (appearing) like an old date stalk. [40] It is not for the sun to reach the moon, nor does the night overtake the day, but each swims in an orbit. [41] And a sign for them is that We carried their forefathers in a laden ship. [42] And We created for them from the likes of it that which they ride. [43] And if We willed, We could drown them; then no helper (responding to their cry) would there be, nor would they be saved—[44] Except as a mercy from Us and provision for a time.

"And a Sign for Them ..."

Within the following *āyahs* are proofs, not only of the Creator's unlimited power and ability but of His unity as reflected in creation. These *āyahs* are truly signs of Allah from Allah. Although they initially draw man's attention to that which is completely familiar to him, they contain information only recently understood and appreciated after scientific research led to new and amazing discoveries. Being the final revelation to mankind, the Qur'an has been made a continuing miracle by Allah containing evidence to be uncovered gradually as men increase in knowledge of their universe.

The Qur'an is not, and was never meant to be, a book of scientific facts, as such. It is a book of guidance, merely mentioning certain realities recognized by men both at the time of revelation and again in later centuries—realities submitted as evidence and proof which cannot be denied. Ironically, the most notable of these proofs have been exposed to the world in recent years by non-believers, who pridc themselves on scientific achievement and who do not consider themselves in need of religion. With the exception of a few honest souls among them who have been guided to faith, the egotism and arrogance of many scientists have prevented them from benefiting from the signs of Allah manifest before their very eyes.

But for those hearts and souls open to the truth, understanding comes easily, and they are seized with awe and reverence. For even that portion of the universe now known to man through observation and calculation is much more complex and mysterious than we can imagine. Undoubtedly, every new discovery in the world of matter, energy, time and space can only increase the believer in faith and humility towards Him Who devised, projected and systematized such a plan and then assigned to mankind his place within it, giving him the noble role of Allah's representative upon the earth.

Some Muslims, although harboring good intentions, have fallen into the error of seeking to "prove" the Qur'an's authenticity with modern scientific findings. In reality, the Qur'an is itself a final statement—the absolute divine criterion by which all other statements and theories can be judged. Conversely, those "facts" accepted by science today are neither final nor absolute.

The scientific miracle of the Qur'an does not lie merely in its allusion to certain physical realities, but more in its advocation of the research, study, thought and contemplation that leads humanity to faith by actual conviction rather than blind acceptance. The Qur'an urges man to consider the signs in all of creation, including his own self, thus giving him guidelines for the sound thinking which leads to correct conclusions. Allah states:

سَنُرِيهِمْ ءَايَٰتِنَا فِى ٱلْءَافَاقِ وَفِىٓ أَنفُسِهِمْ حَتَّىٰ يَتَبَيَّنَ لَهُمْ أَنَّهُ ٱلْحَقُّ ۗ أَوَلَمْ يَكْفِ بِرَبِّكَ أَنَّهُۥ عَلَىٰ كُلِّ شَىْءٍ شَهِيدٌ ﴿٥٣﴾ ﴿فُصِّلَتْ﴾

"We shall show them Our signs in the horizons and within themselves until it becomes evident to them that it is the truth. But then, is it not sufficient that your Lord is witness over all things?" (41:53)

Āyahs 33–35

وَءَايَةٌ لَّهُمُ ٱلْأَرْضُ ٱلْمَيْتَةُ أَحْيَيْنَٰهَا وَأَخْرَجْنَا مِنْهَا حَبًّا
فَمِنْهُ يَأْكُلُونَ ﴿٣٣﴾ وَجَعَلْنَا فِيهَا جَنَّٰتٍ مِّن نَّخِيلٍ
وَأَعْنَٰبٍ وَفَجَّرْنَا فِيهَا مِنَ ٱلْعُيُونِ ﴿٣٤﴾ لِيَأْكُلُوا۟ مِن ثَمَرِهِۦ
وَمَا عَمِلَتْهُ أَيْدِيهِمْ ۖ أَفَلَا يَشْكُرُونَ ﴿٣٥﴾

[33] And a sign for them is the dead earth. We have brought it to life and brought forth from it seeds from which they then eat. [34] And We made therein gardens of date-palms and grapes and caused springs to burst forth therefrom [35] So that they may eat of its fruit. And their hands have not produced it, so will they not give thanks?

The word *āyah* is used here to convey its general meaning of "sign" or "evidence" of a certain truth given by Allah (ﷻ). Thus, an *āyah* (verse) from the Qur'an is included in this general meaning as well, for every Qur'anic *āyah* is a sign from Allah to mankind complementing those signs manifest in the physical universe.

"And a sign for them" who have denied the messengers of Allah, who remain unmoved by the lessons of past generations and who do not understand the point behind the fact mentioned in the previous verse—that they will leave this world never to return—"a sign for them is the dead earth. We have brought it to life." The sign presented is evidence of the Creator, Who recreates and gives life to that which is seemingly dead. The prophets and messengers have imparted such information while inviting mankind to Allah. But, in reality, all creation speaks of Allah, providing countless examples of His creative power.

Here is the earth directly before the eyes of men and under their feet. They see it, in periods of drought, burned and parched,[1] with no signs of life on its surface. Then they see it come alive with green sprouts and small creatures within hours after a life-giving rainfall. Allah describes it thus: "And you see the earth lifeless. Then when We send down upon it water, it quivers and grows" (22:5). The miracle of life reoccurring periodically before the human eye, the production of a tiny seed from which life begins anew, the variation of seeds and grains which give sustenance and nourishment to men as well as other creatures, the atmospheric properties causing suitable conditions for life and growth upon the earth, and the dependence of those conditions upon such external factors as the earth's relationship to the sun—all of these are evidence of an intricate plan devised by a supreme Creator.

Some of the seeds will be eaten, some will be lost due to unfavorable conditions, and some will grow to produce vegetation, fruits and new seeds, by Allah's will. Man might take for granted his provisions from the earth, but if he observes and considers carefully, he cannot fail to appreciate plant life and water which sustains it, knowing

1. In colder climates the earth appears lifeless when frozen over with ice or snow.

that he is completely dependent upon the perpetuation of these blessings for him by Allah (ﷻ):

وَهُوَ ٱلَّذِىٓ أَنزَلَ مِنَ ٱلسَّمَآءِ مَآءً فَأَخْرَجْنَا بِهِۦ نَبَاتَ كُلِّ شَىْءٍ
فَأَخْرَجْنَا مِنْهُ خَضِرًا نُّخْرِجُ مِنْهُ حَبًّا مُّتَرَاكِبًا وَمِنَ ٱلنَّخْلِ مِن
طَلْعِهَا قِنْوَانٌ دَانِيَةٌ وَجَنَّٰتٍ مِّنْ أَعْنَابٍ وَٱلزَّيْتُونَ وَٱلرُّمَّانَ مُشْتَبِهًا
وَغَيْرَ مُتَشَٰبِهٍ ۗ ٱنظُرُوٓا۟ إِلَىٰ ثَمَرِهِۦٓ إِذَآ أَثْمَرَ وَيَنْعِهِۦٓ ۚ إِنَّ فِى ذَٰلِكُمْ
لَءَايَٰتٍ لِّقَوْمٍ يُؤْمِنُونَ ﴿٩٩﴾ ﴿الأنعام﴾

"And it is He Who sends down water from the sky by which We bring out the growth of all things. We produce from it greenery from which We produce seeds arranged in layers. And from the date-palm—from its emerging fruit are clusters hanging low. And (We produce) gardens of grapes and olives and pomegranates, similar yet varied. Observe its fruit when it yields and its ripening. Surely in this are signs for a people who believe." (6:99)[2]

This intricate system was produced not only for the perpetuation of human life upon the earth but for man's enjoyment as well. Whether he eats directly from plant life or from animals dependent upon plant life, his food is a gift from the Sustainer. Men may plant and harvest by His will, but it is His hand, not theirs, that guides the tender sprout up through the darkness of the earth to the light of the sun, strengthens it and stretches it, then decorates its branches

2. See also 13:4.

with leaves and blossoms, and ripens its fruit in preparation for consumption … "so will they not give thanks?" Will they not recognize the favor of Allah, Who has provided everything necessary for their survival and pleasure on earth? Or will they then turn ungratefully from Him to some other object of devotion.

Note: Some *tafsīrs* give an alternative meaning for this *āyah* by considering the word *mā* to mean "what" rather than negation. As such, the *āyah* can be read: "So that they may eat from its fruit and (from) what their hands have produced (*ie.,* planted and harvested)." Both are grammatically correct in Arabic, although most commentators prefer the first meaning.

Āyah 36

سُبۡحَٰنَ ٱلَّذِي خَلَقَ ٱلۡأَزۡوَٰجَ كُلَّهَا مِمَّا تُنۢبِتُ ٱلۡأَرۡضُ وَمِنۡ أَنفُسِهِمۡ وَمِمَّا لَا يَعۡلَمُونَ ٣٦

> [36] Praise be to Him Who created all in pairs—from what the earth grows and from themselves and from that which they do not know.

The phrase *subḥān Allāh* (praise be to Allah) is most often used in the Qur'an to refute those claims which imply that Allah is somehow in need of an associate or intermediary. It means such praise which negates imperfection and confirms that Allah is completely free from any fault or inability ascribed to Him by the ignorant. The word of praise is used here to emphasize an important fact—the regular consistency in creation, which points to the oneness of the Creator. For, in spite of the variations in types and sizes, in appearances and functions, all of creation has the same basis and form—that of duality— while the Creator alone is one.

So praise is due to Allah alone, Who created all things in pairs. These have been categorized in the *āyah* under three headings: Firstly, He has created pairs "from what the earth grows", *ie.,* plant and animal life. Although the Arabs at the time of the Qur'an's revelation had observed that date-palms appear to have a form of sexuality and had put this knowledge to practical use in their orchards, they could not have guessed that other plant forms also contain male and female parts or that new life in every form is dependent upon the coming together of two opposite components.

Secondly, Allah has created mankind in pairs "from themselves", as mentioned in the *āyah*:

وَمِنْ ءَايَـٰتِهِۦٓ أَنْ خَلَقَ لَكُم مِّنْ أَنفُسِكُمْ أَزْوَٰجًا لِّتَسْكُنُوٓا۟ إِلَيْهَا وَجَعَلَ بَيْنَكُم مَّوَدَّةً وَرَحْمَةً ۚ إِنَّ فِى ذَٰلِكَ لَءَايَـٰتٍ لِّقَوْمٍ يَتَفَكَّرُونَ ﴿٢١﴾ ﴿الرُّوم﴾

"And among His signs is that He created for you from yourselves mates that you may find peace with them ..." (30:21)

Thirdly, He has created pairs "from that which they do not know". Until recently it was not known that even lifeless matter is held together by the affinity and attraction of pairs in the form of positive and negative charges. This principle of duality, which governs the existence of our universe in such intricate precision, is mentioned by Allah (ﷻ) in another *āyah:*

وَمِن كُلِّ شَيْءٍ خَلَقْنَا زَوْجَيْنِ لَعَلَّكُمْ تَذَكَّرُونَ ﴿٤٩﴾ ﴿الذاريات﴾

"And from all things We have created two counterparts—that perhaps you will be reminded." (51:49)

Further examples are to be found in various phenomena observed throughout creation. Such opposites as night and day are visible and recognizable to all, while others require a particular appreciation through knowledge gained by means of special instruments or complex calculations. Needless to say, in his quest for information, mankind will continue to discover pairs about which today he has no knowledge.

Āyah 37

وَءَايَةٌ لَّهُمُ ٱلَّيْلُ نَسْلَخُ مِنْهُ ٱلنَّهَارَ فَإِذَا هُم مُّظْلِمُونَ ﴿٣٧﴾

[37] And a sign for them is the night. We strip from it the day, so they are left in darkness.

From the earth, Allah (ﷻ) turns our attention to the heavens, beginning with a phenomenon observed regularly by the earths inhabitants—the approach of nightfall and the disappearance of daylight. The Qur'anic expression here is unique, for it pictures the day as a covering over the night, concealing it. Allah then strips or peels this covering away as the earth turns in its orbit. When remembering that the original state in space is that of darkness and that light from the sun is projected onto the dark earth, one comprehends the accuracy of this description. For when a given point upon the earth turns away from the sun, the light covering its surface is removed, leaving it in its "undressed" state of darkness.

Āyah 38

وَٱلشَّمْسُ تَجْرِى لِمُسْتَقَرٍّ لَّهَا ۚ ذَٰلِكَ تَقْدِيرُ ٱلْعَزِيزِ ٱلْعَلِيمِ ﴿٣٨﴾

[38] And the sun runs on course towards its final destination. That is the calculation of the Almighty, the All-Knowing.

Not long ago it was assumed that the sun, being the nucleus of our solar system, was stationary, merely rotating on its axis. But now it has been shown that our sun, like other stars, is traveling through space in a single direction—rushing headlong at a speed of approximately twenty kilometers per second. Allah (ﷻ) informs us that this phenomenon, as is the case with all creation, is a temporary state which will come to an end. Indeed, the sun will progressively run its course until it reaches a point decreed by Allah (ﷻ). Commentators have offered two explanations concerning this "point":

1. It is a point in space (*ie.,* a resting place). This is also described in several *ḥadīths,* as reported in *Ṣaḥīḥ al-Bukhārī* in which Abū Dharr is asked by

the Prophet (ﷺ), "Do you know where the sun goes when it sets?" and is then informed by him, "It goes to prostrate before its Lord beneath the Throne." A narration by Aḥmad adds: "... where it asks permission to rise again." Ibn Kathīr has explained, "Wherever the sun might be in relation to the earth, it will always be under the Throne of Allah (ﷻ), which covers all of creation as a canopy. It reappears (successively around the globe) after its absence at night, by permission of Allah."

As for the suns prostration, it might be compared to that of other forms of creation which submit obediently to His law, as mentioned in the Qur'an:

﴿وَٱلنَّجْمُ وَٱلشَّجَرُ يَسْجُدَانِ ۝٦﴾ ﴿الرَّحْمَٰن﴾

"And the stars and the trees prostrate themselves." (55:6)

﴿وَلِلَّهِ يَسْجُدُ مَن فِي ٱلسَّمَٰوَٰتِ وَٱلْأَرْضِ طَوْعًا وَكَرْهًا وَظِلَٰلُهُم بِٱلْغُدُوِّ وَٱلْآصَالِ ۝١٥﴾ ﴿الرَّعْد﴾

"And to Allah prostrate themselves all within the heavens and the earth, voluntarily or involuntarily, and (also) their shadows in the morning and afternoon." (13:15)

أَلَمْ تَرَ أَنَّ ٱللَّهَ يَسْجُدُ لَهُۥ مَن فِي ٱلسَّمَٰوَٰتِ وَمَن فِي ٱلْأَرْضِ وَٱلشَّمْسُ وَٱلْقَمَرُ وَٱلنُّجُومُ وَٱلْجِبَالُ وَٱلشَّجَرُ وَٱلدَّوَآبُّ

وَكَثِيرٌ مِّنَ ٱلنَّاسِ ۖ وَكَثِيرٌ حَقَّ عَلَيْهِ ٱلْعَذَابُ ۗ وَمَن يُهِنِ ٱللَّهُ فَمَا
لَهُۥ مِن مُّكْرِمٍ ۚ إِنَّ ٱللَّهَ يَفْعَلُ مَا يَشَآءُ ۩ ﴿١٨﴾ ﴿الحج﴾

"Do you not consider that to Allah prostrates all within the heavens and the earth—the sun, the moon, the stars, the mountains, the trees, the animals and many of the people ...?" (22:18)

2. It is a point in time (*ie.,* the Day of Judgement) when the universe, as we know it, will end, preceding the second creation, as expressed in the words of the Qur'an:

إِذَا ٱلشَّمْسُ كُوِّرَتْ ﴿١﴾ ﴿التكوير﴾

"When the sun is wound up ..." (81:1)

The sun, with its huge, flaming mass which is yet a tiny speck on the outskirts of a vast, expanding universe, is hastening on towards a specific point in time and space—a final destination—drawing its satellites (including our earth) in the same direction and at the same speed. The realization of this fact can only bring one face to face with a certain reality—his total helplessness before the will of the Creator of this entity, Who has informed mankind of His plan and warned him against rebellion. "That is the calculation of the Almighty"—He Who cannot be opposed or prevented from what He wills "The All-Knowing", Who is fully aware of every movement and every stillness.

Āyah 39

وَٱلْقَمَرَ قَدَّرْنَٰهُ مَنَازِلَ حَتَّىٰ عَادَ كَٱلْعُرْجُونِ ٱلْقَدِيمِ ﴿٣٩﴾

[39] And the moon—We have determined for it phases until it returns (appearing) like an old date stalk.

Again man is reminded of an occurrence which he witnesses repeatedly throughout his lifetime—the successive stages of the moon, by which the months are recognized, just as the sun provides the standard of measure for days and nights. As Allah mentions in other *āyahs*:

هُوَ ٱلَّذِى جَعَلَ ٱلشَّمْسَ ضِيَآءً وَٱلْقَمَرَ نُورًا وَقَدَّرَهُۥ مَنَازِلَ لِتَعْلَمُوا۟ عَدَدَ ٱلسِّنِينَ وَٱلْحِسَابَ ۚ مَا خَلَقَ ٱللَّهُ ذَٰلِكَ إِلَّا بِٱلْحَقِّ ۚ يُفَصِّلُ ٱلْءَايَٰتِ لِقَوْمٍ يَعْلَمُونَ ﴿٥﴾ ﴿يونس﴾

"It is He Who has made the sun a shining light and the moon a reflected light and determined for it phases—that you may know the number of years and account (of time) …" (10:5)

وَجَعَلْنَا ٱلَّيْلَ وَٱلنَّهَارَ ءَايَتَيْنِ ۖ فَمَحَوْنَآ ءَايَةَ ٱلَّيْلِ وَجَعَلْنَآ ءَايَةَ ٱلنَّهَارِ مُبْصِرَةً لِّتَبْتَغُوا۟ فَضْلًا مِّن رَّبِّكُمْ وَلِتَعْلَمُوا۟ عَدَدَ ٱلسِّنِينَ وَٱلْحِسَابَ ۚ وَكُلَّ شَىْءٍ فَصَّلْنَٰهُ تَفْصِيلًا ﴿١٢﴾ ﴿الإسراء﴾

"And We have made the night and day (as) two signs. Then We erased the sign of the night and made the sign of the day visible—that you may seek favors from your Lord and know the number of years and account (of time). And everything We have set forth in complete detail." (17:12)

۞ يَسْـَٔلُونَكَ عَنِ ٱلْأَهِلَّةِ ۖ قُلْ هِىَ مَوَٰقِيتُ لِلنَّاسِ وَٱلْحَجِّ ۗ وَلَيْسَ ٱلْبِرُّ
بِأَن تَأْتُوا۟ ٱلْبُيُوتَ مِن ظُهُورِهَا وَلَٰكِنَّ ٱلْبِرَّ مَنِ ٱتَّقَىٰ ۗ وَأْتُوا۟ ٱلْبُيُوتَ
مِنْ أَبْوَٰبِهَا ۚ وَٱتَّقُوا۟ ٱللَّهَ لَعَلَّكُمْ تُفْلِحُونَ ﴿١٨٩﴾ ﴿البقرة﴾

"They ask you about the new moons. Say, They are (to determine) times for the people and for *ḥajj* ..." (2:189)

The moon is born as a crescent, and then it grows night after night until it becomes full and bright. Then it begins to decrease until it is once more a crescent shape—but this time with a difference. For the new moon appears with a glow of freshness and youth, but the waning moon fades as in old age, reminding the observer of a dried date stalk which has withered into a thin, sickle shape. It is not by chance that the Qur'an uses this particular description.[3]

Āyah 40

لَا ٱلشَّمْسُ يَنۢبَغِى لَهَآ أَن تُدْرِكَ ٱلْقَمَرَ وَلَا ٱلَّيْلُ سَابِقُ
ٱلنَّهَارِ ۚ وَكُلٌّ فِى فَلَكٍ يَسْبَحُونَ ﴿٤٠﴾

[40] It is not for the sun to reach the moon, nor does the night overtake the day, but each swims in an orbit.

3. *Fī Ẓilāl al-Qur'ān*, p. 2969.

Up until recent times the sun and the moon seemed to the earth's inhabitants to be following a similar course—each in turn—rising in the east and setting in the west. The frequent appearance of the moon during daylight hours gives an additional allusion of nearness at times.

Yet Allah (ﷻ) affirmed in the Qur'an long before the advent of modern science that the sun cannot make contact with the moon, nor can the sequence of night and day be affected, since each of these bodies is restricted to its own orbit, unable to escape or to alter the path ordained for it—neither transgressing its limit nor falling behind.

Besides the precision of their orbits, the vast distances between each of the heavenly bodies serves to offset the effect of gravity, which would otherwise pull them into a collision course. These distances are hard to imagine even today. The moon is a mere 387,000 kilometers from our earth, while the sun is 150 million kilometers away. Yet these figures are insignificant when compared to the distance between our galaxy and that nearest to us, estimated at about 167 million million kilometers or four light years.[4] Between the cluster to which our galaxy belongs and that next to it is a distance of some fifty million light years. These clusters have been observed in every direction that one can look into space—moving rapidly away from us and from each other:

﴿ وَٱلسَّمَآءَ بَنَيْنَٰهَا بِأَيْيدٍ وَإِنَّا لَمُوسِعُونَ ﴿٤٧﴾ ﴾ ﴿الذاريات﴾

4. A light year is the distance light travels through space in one year at the speed of almost 300,000 kilometers per second.

"And the heavenly structure—We have constructed it with strength, and it is We Who expand (it)." (51:47)

So for as long as the Creator wills, great distances and precision of orbits will prevent the sun from reaching the moon or the night overtaking the day. The orbits themselves are described by the word *falak* which was explained by Ibn 'Abbās and others, as resembling "the cog wheels of a weaving tool commonly used at that time, which do not rotate except conjointly in a mutual relationship". The movement of each body in its orbit is further described in the Qur'an as "swimming". Such are the realities revealed by the Creator of the heavens and the earth to His unlettered prophet over fourteen centuries ago:

۞ إِنَّ ٱللَّهَ يُمْسِكُ ٱلسَّمَٰوَٰتِ وَٱلْأَرْضَ أَن تَزُولَا ۚ وَلَئِن زَالَتَآ إِنْ أَمْسَكَهُمَا مِنْ أَحَدٍ مِّنۢ بَعْدِهِۦٓ ۚ إِنَّهُۥ كَانَ حَلِيمًا غَفُورًا ﴿٤١﴾ ﴿فَاطِر﴾

"Surely does Allah hold the heavens and the earth, lest they cease. And if they should cease, none can hold them after Him ..." (35:41)

Āyah 41

وَءَايَةٌ لَّهُمْ أَنَّا حَمَلْنَا ذُرِّيَّتَهُمْ فِى ٱلْفُلْكِ ٱلْمَشْحُونِ ﴿٤١﴾

[41] And a sign for them is that We carried their forefathers in a laden ship.

In a subtle allusion to a common law governing the floating of stars and planets in space and that of ships on water, Allah (ﷻ) turns our attention to yet another sign—the Ark which carried Prophet Nūḥ (Noah), and the few believers among his people, over the flood waters to safety. For it was under divine inspiration and instruction that he constructed this first ship which served as a model for later vessels.

We are reminded that not only did Allah favor man by teaching him how to cross rivers and seas but also that He saved the faithful who had accompanied Nūḥ in the Ark, making them the forefathers of all men to be born after them. The waters which had destroyed the evildoers were at once a blessing for the believers by Allah's will. Indeed, by His will, all favors are granted and all knowledge is gained. Referring to this event in the Qur'an, He addresses mankind:

إِنَّا لَمَّا طَغَا ٱلْمَآءُ حَمَلْنَـٰكُمْ فِى ٱلْجَارِيَةِ ﴿١١﴾ لِنَجْعَلَهَا لَكُمْ تَذْكِرَةً وَتَعِيَهَآ أُذُنٌ وَٰعِيَةٌ ﴿١٢﴾ ﴿الحاقة﴾

"Verily, when the water overflowed, We carried you in the (moving) ship—that We might make it a reminder for you and that it might be understood by understanding ears." (69:11–12)

Thus, as an additional favor, all believers can benefit from the lessons of the past related to them by Allah (ﷻ).

Āyah 42

وَخَلَقْنَا لَهُم مِّن مِّثْلِهِۦ مَا يَرْكَبُونَ ﴿٤٢﴾

[42] And We created for them from the likes of it that which they ride.

Although one interpretation states that this creation refers to camels or other beasts of burden, the more generally accepted explanation is that it means those ships which were later fashioned from the pattern of the first Ark. Since the source of all human knowledge and ability is Allah, He aptly describes man's work as His creation. In the words of Prophet Ibrāhīm:

﴿وَٱللَّهُ خَلَقَكُمْ وَمَا تَعْمَلُونَ ﴿٩٦﴾﴾ (الصَّافَّات)

"And Allah created you and that which you do." (37:96)

Āyah 43

وَإِن نَّشَأْ نُغْرِقْهُمْ فَلَا صَرِيخَ لَهُمْ وَلَا هُمْ يُنقَذُونَ ﴿٤٣﴾

> [43] And if We willed We could drown them; then no helper (responding to their cry) would there be, nor would they be saved.

Here is a further reminder to those who through pride and confidence in their own achievements forget themselves and their debt to Allah. For it is He Who has given them life and sustenance and then knowledge and skill, enabling them to sail the seas in search of His bounty. Yet He could just as well withdraw His protection at any instant, exposing them to terror and sudden death.[5] Every individual is safeguarded whether on land or at sea simply because Allah (ﷻ) has willed his existence to continue for a specified period "to test you as to which of you is best in deed."[6]

---

5. See 17:66–70.
6. Sūrah al-Mulk, (67:2).

Āyah 44

إِلَّا رَحْمَةً مِّنَّا وَمَتَـٰعًا إِلَىٰ حِينٍ ﴿٤٤﴾

[44] Except as a mercy from Us and provision for a time.

Were it not for the mercy of Allah, no one could survive the violent and all-encompassing forces of nature. If not for the mercy of Allah, life could not continue. Yet He grants this extension to provide every soul with opportunities for accepting the truth, for repenting from sin or for increasing in righteousness until the appointed time for return unto Him.

But in spite of those mentioned and of countless other great signs, mankind remains in a state of unconsciousness, forgetting Allah except in periods of anxiety and distress:

فَإِذَا رَكِبُوا۟ فِى ٱلْفُلْكِ دَعَوُا۟ ٱللَّهَ مُخْلِصِينَ لَهُ ٱلدِّينَ فَلَمَّا نَجَّىٰهُمْ إِلَى ٱلْبَرِّ إِذَا هُمْ يُشْرِكُونَ ﴿٦٥﴾ لِيَكْفُرُوا۟ بِمَآ ءَاتَيْنَـٰهُمْ وَلِيَتَمَتَّعُوا۟ فَسَوْفَ يَعْلَمُونَ ﴿٦٦﴾ ﴿العنكبوت﴾

"Then if they board a ship, they supplicate Allah, sincere in religion (*ie.,* devotion) to Him. But when He delivers them to land, they associate others with Him. So let them deny what We have granted them, and let them enjoy themselves—for they are going to know." (29:65–66)

ٱلَّذِى خَلَقَ ٱلْمَوْتَ وَٱلْحَيَوٰةَ لِيَبْلُوَكُمْ أَيُّكُمْ أَحْسَنُ عَمَلًا ۚ وَهُوَ ٱلْعَزِيزُ ٱلْغَفُورُ ﴿٢﴾ ﴿الملك﴾

ĀYAHS 45–54

وَإِذَا قِيلَ لَهُمُ ٱتَّقُواْ مَا بَيۡنَ أَيۡدِيكُمۡ وَمَا خَلۡفَكُمۡ لَعَلَّكُمۡ تُرۡحَمُونَ ﴿٤٥﴾
وَمَا تَأۡتِيهِم مِّنۡ ءَايَةٖ مِّنۡ ءَايَٰتِ رَبِّهِمۡ إِلَّا كَانُواْ عَنۡهَا مُعۡرِضِينَ ﴿٤٦﴾
وَإِذَا قِيلَ لَهُمۡ أَنفِقُواْ مِمَّا رَزَقَكُمُ ٱللَّهُ قَالَ ٱلَّذِينَ كَفَرُواْ لِلَّذِينَ
ءَامَنُوٓاْ أَنُطۡعِمُ مَن لَّوۡ يَشَآءُ ٱللَّهُ أَطۡعَمَهُۥٓ إِنۡ أَنتُمۡ إِلَّا فِي ضَلَٰلٖ
مُّبِينٖ ﴿٤٧﴾ وَيَقُولُونَ مَتَىٰ هَٰذَا ٱلۡوَعۡدُ إِن كُنتُمۡ صَٰدِقِينَ ﴿٤٨﴾ مَا
يَنظُرُونَ إِلَّا صَيۡحَةٗ وَٰحِدَةٗ تَأۡخُذُهُمۡ وَهُمۡ يَخِصِّمُونَ ﴿٤٩﴾ فَلَا
يَسۡتَطِيعُونَ تَوۡصِيَةٗ وَلَآ إِلَىٰٓ أَهۡلِهِمۡ يَرۡجِعُونَ ﴿٥٠﴾ وَنُفِخَ فِي
ٱلصُّورِ فَإِذَا هُم مِّنَ ٱلۡأَجۡدَاثِ إِلَىٰ رَبِّهِمۡ يَنسِلُونَ ﴿٥١﴾ قَالُواْ
يَٰوَيۡلَنَا مَنۢ بَعَثَنَا مِن مَّرۡقَدِنَاۜۗ هَٰذَا مَا وَعَدَ ٱلرَّحۡمَٰنُ وَصَدَقَ
ٱلۡمُرۡسَلُونَ ﴿٥٢﴾ إِن كَانَتۡ إِلَّا صَيۡحَةٗ وَٰحِدَةٗ فَإِذَا هُمۡ جَمِيعٞ
لَّدَيۡنَا مُحۡضَرُونَ ﴿٥٣﴾ فَٱلۡيَوۡمَ لَا تُظۡلَمُ نَفۡسٞ شَيۡـٔٗا وَلَا تُجۡزَوۡنَ إِلَّا
مَا كُنتُمۡ تَعۡمَلُونَ ﴿٥٤﴾

[45] But when it is said to them, "Beware of that before you and that after you so perhaps you will receive mercy ..." [46] And no sign comes to them from the signs of their Lord except that they turn away therefrom. [47]

And when it is said to them, "Spend from that with which Allah has provided you," the unbelievers say to the believers, "Should we feed him whom if Allah had willed He would have fed? You are not but in manifest error." [48] And they say, "When is this promise, if you should be truthful?" [49] They await not except one blast; it will seize them while they are disputing. [50] Then they will not be able to give any instruction, nor can they return to their people. [51] And the Horn shall be blown; then (immediately) they will hasten from their graves to their Lord. [52] They will say, "O ruined are we! Who has raised us up again from our beds?! This is what al-Raḥmān had promised, and the messengers have told the truth." [53] It is not but one blast and they are all brought present before Us. [54] So today no soul will be wronged at all, and you will not be penalized except for what you used to do.

Āyah 45

وَإِذَا قِيلَ لَهُمُ ٱتَّقُواْ مَا بَيْنَ أَيْدِيكُمْ وَمَا خَلْفَكُمْ لَعَلَّكُمْ تُرْحَمُونَ ﴿٤٥﴾

> [45] But when it is said to them, "Beware of that before you and that after you so perhaps you will receive mercy ..."

"That before you" is expressed in Arabic literally as "that between your hands", *ie.,* what you already have. Early scholars have defined "that before" and "that after" as follows:

That before	That after
• Past sins	• Future sins
• Lessons from history	• What will be in the Hereafter
• The portion of life already lived	• What remains of one's life span
• This world	• The punishment of the Hereafter
• What is apparent	• What is concealed

Although the sentence in this *āyah* appears incomplete, its conclusion is understood grammatically as "... they ignore the warning", the interpretation being based upon the *āyah* which follows it.

From among the Creator's many manifest signs, He has given in the previous verses a few examples which are sufficient to evoke wonder and apprehension in the heart. But persons blinded by worldly distractions and self-obsession will not even notice them, much less reflect upon their significance. In His mercy, however, Allah has not left even such souls as these without guidance but has sent messengers to point out His signs in clear language and invite them to Him. Yet despite this great favor to mankind, there remain many who refuse their Lord's invitation to mercy, reject His message and ignore His warnings.

Āyah 46

وَمَا تَأۡتِيهِم مِّنۡ ءَايَةٖ مِّنۡ ءَايَٰتِ رَبِّهِمۡ إِلَّا كَانُواْ عَنۡهَا مُعۡرِضِينَ ﴿٤٦﴾

[46] And no sign comes to them from the signs of their Lord except that they turn away therefrom.

In spite of the countless signs of the power, ability and unity of Allah before their very eyes, the disbelievers will continue to take them for granted, if indeed they notice them at all. Allah confirms in a similar *āyah:*

وَكَأَيِّن مِّنْ ءَايَةٍ فِي ٱلسَّمَـٰوَٰتِ وَٱلْأَرْضِ يَمُرُّونَ عَلَيْهَا وَهُمْ عَنْهَا مُعْرِضُونَ ﴿١٠٥﴾ ﴿يوسف﴾

"And how many signs in the heavens and the earth do they pass by, yet they are turning away from them." (12:105)

They will neither reflect upon their significance nor take seriously those who point it out to them. They will write off those signs as mere accidents of nature or as creations brought into being without purpose. Even their own existence is seen by them as meaningless beyond the joys and hardships of this earthly life; thus they refuse to heed any suggestion of caution, while exploiting any and every opportunity for pleasure or worldly gain.

Āyah 47

وَإِذَا قِيلَ لَهُمْ أَنفِقُوا۟ مِمَّا رَزَقَكُمُ ٱللَّهُ قَالَ ٱلَّذِينَ كَفَرُوا۟ لِلَّذِينَ ءَامَنُوٓا۟ أَنُطْعِمُ مَن لَّوْ يَشَآءُ ٱللَّهُ أَطْعَمَهُۥٓ إِنْ أَنتُمْ إِلَّا فِي ضَلَـٰلٍ مُّبِينٍ ﴿٤٧﴾

[47] And when it is said to them, "Spend from that with which Allah has provided you," the unbelievers say to the believers, "Should we feed him whom if Allah had willed He would have fed? You are not but in manifest error."

Here is a scene from the past and the present. This *āyah* reveals a picture of the selfish, materialistic mentality which considers the well-off as deserving of Allah's favor while those of little means are seen as less worthy. Moreover, there is an insolent attempt to shift the responsibility and blame for the condition of the needy onto Allah (ﷻ), just as the polytheists did, saying: "If Allah had willed, we would not have worshipped anything other than Him—neither we nor our forefathers ...".[1] But in their pretense of wit and cleverness with the assertion that one cannot tamper with fate, the shortsighted souls again overlook the fact that Allah has willed human responsibility and accountability for all that He has commanded.

Those who decline to share their wealth, assuming that they are within their right and that they are not responsible for the plight of others, suggest that the condition of poverty is due only to laziness and incompetence. Yet inactivity, far from being an inborn trait, has been shown to be a direct result of hunger, disease and misery. Poor nutrition affects not only brain development in fetuses and children but production capacity in adults as well. Nevertheless, in recent years the destruction of surplus food stocks in Western Europe and America while millions in

---

1. Sūrah al-Naḥl, (16:35)

وَقَالَ ٱلَّذِينَ أَشْرَكُواْ لَوْ شَآءَ ٱللَّهُ مَا عَبَدْنَا مِن دُونِهِۦ مِن شَيْءٍ نَّحْنُ وَلَآ ءَابَآؤُنَا وَلَا حَرَّمْنَا مِن دُونِهِۦ مِن شَيْءٍۚ كَذَٰلِكَ فَعَلَ ٱلَّذِينَ مِن قَبْلِهِمْۚ فَهَلْ عَلَى ٱلرُّسُلِ إِلَّا ٱلْبَلَٰغُ ٱلْمُبِينُ ﴿٣٥﴾

third-world countries are dying of hunger has been excused with the claim that supplying the needs of those people would destroy their motive for becoming self-sufficient! It has been estimated that a mere portion of the surplus grain fed to livestock in western countries could save all those who are dying from hunger throughout the entire underdeveloped world. As 'Alī bin Abī Ṭālib aptly said, "No poor man goes hungry except by what a rich man withholds." But food has became an instrument in the hands of the wealthy, its political utilization deemed more important than its humanitarian one.

In materialistic societies it is readily observed that the most selfish are the most successful. The world does not presently suffer from a lack of resources—only a lack of balance in distribution. But the situation will not be remedied by those who perpetrate it—those whose only aim is profit and accumulation of wealth, those who flaunt statistics while casting aside religious ethics, saying to whoever should encourage generosity and assistance to the hungry, "You are not but in manifest error."

So much for the injustice of the unbelievers. This is to be expected. But what is to be said of the Muslim community?

Islam treats the issue of economic imbalance in a unique manner with both preventative and corrective measures—not simply with advice or encouragement, but with legislation. After establishing a system that guarantees just opportunities for every individual and makes work obligatory for every able-bodied man, it leaves human activity to take its course. It then counteracts any possible ill effects by requiring expenditure on the part of those who have excess until the minimum needs of all are met. In emergency situations, *ṣadaqah,* normally a charity beyond the duty of *zakāh,* becomes obligatory as well.

But unhappily, many of those who call themselves Muslims today have taken on the attitudes condemned in the Qur'an and attributed to unbelievers. While large Muslim populations in Africa and Asia facing drought, famine, disease and death find no relief except occasionally through western aid or that of the Christian missionaries, their prosperous brothers, whose duty it is to take part in the economic uplift of the poor, continue to seek endless acquisitions and short-lived pleasures which they consider essential to their own well-being. Some even go so far as to assert that Allah must be punishing the stricken ones for their sins, as if they themselves were faultless!

Have they forgotten that it is Allah Who has provided them with all that they possess and has, in fact, created them and all that they possess? Are they unmindful that He is able at any time He wills to reverse their fortunes or to utterly destroy them? That all of their worldly possessions as well as they themselves will one day return to Him Who created them? That they will be stripped of ownership; their wealth will then be only in terms of righteous deeds and what they had once spent from their property for the pleasure of Allah? And that all which was withheld unlawfully and unjustly will then become an inescapable and suffocating burden around their necks on the Day of

Judgement?[2] Concerning this, the Prophet (ﷺ) once said, "It is not poverty that I fear for you, but I fear that the earth with its comforts will be spread out for you as it was spread for those before you, that you will covet it as they coveted it, and that it will destroy you as it destroyed them."[3]

This world is but a trial—for the rich as well as for the poor. When the sinners are asked in the Hereafter about what led them into Hellfire, they will list among the causes:

﴿وَلَمْ نَكُ نُطْعِمُ ٱلْمِسْكِينَ ۝٤٤﴾ ﴿المدثر﴾

"And we used not to feed the poor." (74:44)

But there will be others of Allah's servants who had done so, saying:

﴿إِنَّمَا نُطْعِمُكُمْ لِوَجْهِ ٱللَّهِ لَا نُرِيدُ مِنكُمْ جَزَآءً وَلَا شُكُورًا ۝٩﴾ ﴿الإنسان﴾

"We feed you for (the acceptance of) Allah. We wish not from you reward nor thanks." (76:9)

Those are among the companions of Paradise.

During the caliphate of 'Umar bin al-Khaṭṭāb, drought struck the Arabian peninsula while the area to the north was suffering from plague. 'Umar attacked the problem of hunger effectively, never once submitting to the claim that fate is unalterable. Mobilizing food supplies from Basrah and from Egypt, he personally supervised distribution, temporarily suspended the legally prescribed punishment for theft (fearing that some might steal out of need) and postponed *zakāh* collection. He himself refrained from

2. See 3:180.
3. Al-Bukhārī and Muslim.

eating more than the minimum requirement and prayed with the people for rain and alleviation of their condition. He later ordered a canal to be dug between the Nile and the Red Sea to facilitate the transfer of supplies in the future. Thus, acutely aware of his responsibility before Allah, 'Umar fought against fate with fate, in obedience to Him with the certain knowledge that exertion to change existing adverse conditions is a noble act of worship.

Allah addresses His servants with these words:

هَٰٓأَنتُمْ هَٰٓؤُلَآءِ تُدْعَوْنَ لِتُنفِقُوا۟ فِى سَبِيلِ ٱللَّهِ فَمِنكُم مَّن يَبْخَلُ ۖ
وَمَن يَبْخَلْ فَإِنَّمَا يَبْخَلُ عَن نَّفْسِهِۦ ۚ وَٱللَّهُ ٱلْغَنِىُّ وَأَنتُمُ ٱلْفُقَرَآءُ ۚ وَإِن
تَتَوَلَّوْا۟ يَسْتَبْدِلْ قَوْمًا غَيْرَكُمْ ثُمَّ لَا يَكُونُوٓا۟ أَمْثَٰلَكُم ﴿٣٨﴾ ﴿محمد﴾

"Here you are—those invited to spend in the way of Allah but among you are some who withhold (from greed). And whoever withholds only withholds (benefit) from himself, and Allah is free of need, while it is you who are in need. If you turn away (in refusal), He will replace you with another people. Then they will not be like you." (47:38)

Āyah 48

وَيَقُولُونَ مَتَىٰ هَٰذَا ٱلْوَعْدُ إِن كُنتُمْ صَٰدِقِينَ ﴿٤٨﴾

[48] And they say, "When is this promise, if you should be truthful?"

These same words have been repeated in five other Sūrahs.[4]

4. See 10:48; 21:38; 27:71; 34:29 and 67:25.

They reflect doubt in the hearts of those who challenge the messengers concerning the Hour of Judgement. Their question is not a request for information but merely a denial of the fact that it will ever come. It shows outright disbelief, as Allah confirms:

يَسْتَعْجِلُ بِهَا ٱلَّذِينَ لَا يُؤْمِنُونَ بِهَا ۖ وَٱلَّذِينَ ءَامَنُوا۟ مُشْفِقُونَ مِنْهَا وَيَعْلَمُونَ أَنَّهَا ٱلْحَقُّ ۗ أَلَآ إِنَّ ٱلَّذِينَ يُمَارُونَ فِى ٱلسَّاعَةِ لَفِى ضَلَٰلٍۭ بَعِيدٍ ﴿١٨﴾ ﴿الشورى﴾

"Those who do not believe in it call for its immediate onset, but those who believe are fearful of it and know that it is the truth …" (42:18)

Since Allah does not disclose the time of Resurrection, the disbelievers attempt to weaken the position of those who warn of it by demanding an answer they cannot give. But He supplies the appropriate answer to their insolence in the following *āyahs*—informing them not *when*, but *how* it will be.

Āyahs 49–50

مَا يَنظُرُونَ إِلَّا صَيْحَةً وَٰحِدَةً تَأْخُذُهُمْ وَهُمْ يَخِصِّمُونَ ﴿٤٩﴾ فَلَا يَسْتَطِيعُونَ تَوْصِيَةً وَلَآ إِلَىٰٓ أَهْلِهِمْ يَرْجِعُونَ ﴿٥٠﴾

[49] They await not except one blast; it will seize them while they are disputing. [50] Then they will not be able to give any instruction, nor can they return to their people.

To those who question the promise of Allah comes the answer in a few words depicting a terrible scene—one dreadful blast[5] which ends all activity upon the earth. There will be no further opportunity for repentance or for action of any kind. At the command of Allah, the angel, Isrāfīl, will blow into the Horn, striking every living thing with terror and then death. The blast will come suddenly without warning while the people are in their markets going about their daily affairs, arguing and disputing as usual.

There will be no chance for counsel and no contact with families. Life will be ended utterly and completely and with it the temporary period of freewill and ability granted to man by Allah (ﷻ). The devastating blast not only terminates life on earth but signals the dissolution of the universe as a whole so that it may be replaced by a new creation suitable for the next life. How futile now are the petty schemes of men. How helpless is all creation before the divine will.

Āyah 51

وَنُفِخَ فِي ٱلصُّورِ فَإِذَا هُم مِّنَ ٱلْأَجْدَاثِ إِلَىٰ رَبِّهِمْ يَنسِلُونَ ﴿٥١﴾

[51] And the Horn shall be blown; then (immediately) they will hasten from their graves to their Lord.

5. The word *ṣayḥah,* translated as "blast" in this context, carries the additional meaning of "a sharp cry or shriek".

This is the blast signaling the Resurrection, whereupon all creatures will be brought back to life on a newly created earth. No longer in control of their own affairs, men will awaken to find themselves being assembled, all generations together, willingly or unwillingly, for the Judgement. They will at once be expelled from under the earth's surface and hurry on towards their Lord, powerless to resist.

In the Qur'an, Allah (ﷻ) describes it thus:

مَّا خَلْقُكُمْ وَلَا بَعْثُكُمْ إِلَّا كَنَفْسٍ وَاحِدَةٍ ۗ إِنَّ ٱللَّهَ سَمِيعٌۢ بَصِيرٌ ﴿٢٨﴾ ﴿لقمان﴾

"Your creation and resurrection are not except as that of a single soul ..." (31:28)

خُشَّعًا أَبْصَٰرُهُمْ يَخْرُجُونَ مِنَ ٱلْأَجْدَاثِ كَأَنَّهُمْ جَرَادٌ مُّنتَشِرٌ ﴿٧﴾ ﴿القمر﴾

"They come out of the graves as if they were locusts spreading." (54:7)

Ibn Kathīr has explained, "On the Day of Judgement the earth will be exchanged for another earth and the heavens (as well), and the dead will emerge alive from their graves by the command of Allah and by His call to them. For He said:

وَمِنْ ءَايَٰتِهِۦٓ أَن تَقُومَ ٱلسَّمَآءُ وَٱلْأَرْضُ بِأَمْرِهِۦ ۚ ثُمَّ إِذَا دَعَاكُمْ دَعْوَةً مِّنَ ٱلْأَرْضِ إِذَآ أَنتُمْ تَخْرُجُونَ ﴿٢٥﴾ ﴿الروم﴾

"… Then when He calls you by a single call from the earth, behold, you (straightway) come forth." (30:25)

Āyah 52

قَالُواْ يَـٰوَيۡلَنَا مَنۢ بَعَثَنَا مِن مَّرۡقَدِنَاۜ هَـٰذَا مَا وَعَدَ ٱلرَّحۡمَـٰنُ
وَصَدَقَ ٱلۡمُرۡسَلُونَ ﴿٥٢﴾

> [52] They will say, "O ruined are we! Who has raised us up again from our beds?! This is what al-Raḥmān had promised; and the messengers have told the truth."

Those who had insisted during their earthly lives that death is final and scoffed at the concept of Afterlife are in a state of shock and dismay upon finding themselves reawakened in a second creation. First wondering in amazement how this came about, they cry out, "Who has raised us up from the graves in which we have lain since death?" Ibn Kathīr has commented that this statement does not mean they had been resting peacefully all that time but only that the punishment of the grave which precedes the punishment of the Hellfire will be as a dream in comparison to the awesome reality of the new life.

Realizing that everything they had once denied and failed to prepare for is now coming true, the evildoers are seized with dread and apprehension: "This is what al-Raḥmān had promised, and the messengers have told the truth."

Commentators have allowed two interpretations concerning this last exclamation:

1. The angels or the believers answer the bewildered questioners by informing them that what is presently taking place is none but the fulfillment of Allah's promise.
2. The questioners themselves now remember the divine message that they had rejected and can only bear witness that they had indeed been warned.

What can await them at this point except the justice they had once thought they would escape?

Āyah 53

إِن كَانَتْ إِلَّا صَيْحَةً وَاحِدَةً فَإِذَا هُمْ جَمِيعٌ لَّدَيْنَا مُحْضَرُونَ ﴿٥٣﴾

[53] It is not but one blast and they are all brought present before Us.

Allah (ﷻ) confirms that there will be no delay, for as soon as life is restored to the dead, they will be brought forth before their Lord for judgement. All of this will take place during a single blast of the Horn or at one command from Allah:

﴿فَإِنَّمَا هِيَ زَجْرَةٌ وَاحِدَةٌ ﴿١٣﴾ فَإِذَا هُم بِالسَّاهِرَةِ ﴿١٤﴾﴾ (النازعات)

"It is only a single shout and they will be (alert) upon the earth's surface." (79:13–14)

Resurrection as described by Allah in the Qur'an is the logical conclusion to the drama of earthly life. Without it there would be no purpose in His creation of man as a reasoning, responsible being or in giving him freedom of will and action. Furthermore, there would be no need for messengers to convey His guidance and warning. But as Allah reminds them in His reproach to those who rejected faith:

أَفَحَسِبْتُمْ أَنَّمَا خَلَقْنَـٰكُمْ عَبَثًا وَأَنَّكُمْ إِلَيْنَا لَا تُرْجَعُونَ ﴿١١٥﴾ ﴿المؤمنون﴾

"Did you think that We had only created you uselessly and that you would not be returned to Us?" (23:115)

Āyah 54

فَٱلْيَوْمَ لَا تُظْلَمُ نَفْسٌ شَيْـًٔا وَلَا تُجْزَوْنَ إِلَّا مَا كُنتُمْ تَعْمَلُونَ ﴿٥٤﴾

> [54] So today no soul will be wronged at all, and you will not be penalized except for what you used to do.

On this day (*ie.,* the Day of Judgement) no soul will be treated unjustly, whether righteous or rebellious. No one will be deprived of the good he earned, and no soul shall bear the burden of another. No punishment will be greater than deserved, and each will be compensated with exact justice. This is part of Allah's mercy to all creation in general. But the believers shall have the additional mercy of forgiveness for minor sins and entrance into Paradise.

Ibn 'Abbās reported that the Prophet (ﷺ) said, "Allah has recorded the good and the bad deeds. Whoever intends a good deed but does not do it—Allah records it as a complete good deed. But if he intends it and does it, Allah records it as ten good deeds up to seven hundred times, to many times over that. And if he intends a bad deed but does not do it, Allah records it as a complete good deed. And if he intends it and does it, Allah records it as one bad deed."[6]

6. Al-Bukhārī and Muslim.

ĀYAHS 55–68

إِنَّ أَصْحَٰبَ ٱلْجَنَّةِ ٱلْيَوْمَ فِى شُغُلٍ فَٰكِهُونَ ﴿٥٥﴾ هُمْ وَأَزْوَٰجُهُمْ
فِى ظِلَٰلٍ عَلَى ٱلْأَرَآئِكِ مُتَّكِـُٔونَ ﴿٥٦﴾ لَهُمْ فِيهَا فَٰكِهَةٌ وَلَهُم مَّا
يَدَّعُونَ ﴿٥٧﴾ سَلَٰمٌ قَوْلًا مِّن رَّبٍّ رَّحِيمٍ ﴿٥٨﴾ وَٱمْتَٰزُوا۟ ٱلْيَوْمَ أَيُّهَا
ٱلْمُجْرِمُونَ ﴿٥٩﴾ أَلَمْ أَعْهَدْ إِلَيْكُمْ يَٰبَنِىٓ ءَادَمَ أَن لَّا تَعْبُدُوا۟
ٱلشَّيْطَٰنَ ۖ إِنَّهُۥ لَكُمْ عَدُوٌّ مُّبِينٌ ﴿٦٠﴾ وَأَنِ ٱعْبُدُونِى ۚ هَٰذَا صِرَٰطٌ
مُّسْتَقِيمٌ ﴿٦١﴾ وَلَقَدْ أَضَلَّ مِنكُمْ جِبِلًّا كَثِيرًا ۖ أَفَلَمْ تَكُونُوا۟
تَعْقِلُونَ ﴿٦٢﴾ هَٰذِهِۦ جَهَنَّمُ ٱلَّتِى كُنتُمْ تُوعَدُونَ ﴿٦٣﴾ ٱصْلَوْهَا
ٱلْيَوْمَ بِمَا كُنتُمْ تَكْفُرُونَ ﴿٦٤﴾ ٱلْيَوْمَ نَخْتِمُ عَلَىٰٓ أَفْوَٰهِهِمْ
وَتُكَلِّمُنَآ أَيْدِيهِمْ وَتَشْهَدُ أَرْجُلُهُم بِمَا كَانُوا۟ يَكْسِبُونَ ﴿٦٥﴾ وَلَوْ نَشَآءُ
لَطَمَسْنَا عَلَىٰٓ أَعْيُنِهِمْ فَٱسْتَبَقُوا۟ ٱلصِّرَٰطَ فَأَنَّىٰ يُبْصِرُونَ ﴿٦٦﴾ وَلَوْ
نَشَآءُ لَمَسَخْنَٰهُمْ عَلَىٰ مَكَانَتِهِمْ فَمَا ٱسْتَطَٰعُوا۟ مُضِيًّا وَلَا
يَرْجِعُونَ ﴿٦٧﴾ وَمَن نُّعَمِّرْهُ نُنَكِّسْهُ فِى ٱلْخَلْقِ ۖ أَفَلَا يَعْقِلُونَ ﴿٦٨﴾

[55] Indeed the companions of Paradise shall that Day have joy in all they do—[56] They and their spouses, in shade, reclining on thrones. [57] For them therein is

fruit and whatever they should call for, [58] (And) 'Peace," a salutation from a merciful Lord. [59] But stand apart today, you criminals. [60] Did I not enjoin upon you, O children of Adam, that you should not worship Shayṭān, for certainly he is to you a manifest enemy, [61] And (that you) worship Me? This is a straight path. [62] And he had (already) led astray from among you much of creation, so did you not have intelligence? [63] This is the Hellfire which you were promised. [64] Burn therein today for what you used to deny. [65] That day We will seal up their mouths, and their hands will speak to Us, and their feet will testify about what they used to earn. [66] Yet if We willed; We could have done away with their eyes, and they would race to reach the path, but how could they see? [67] And if We willed, We could have deformed them, (paralyzing them) in their places so they would neither be able to proceed on, nor could they return. [68] And he to whom We grant long life We reverse in creation; so will they not understand?

Āyahs 55–58

إِنَّ أَصْحَٰبَ ٱلْجَنَّةِ ٱلْيَوْمَ فِى شُغُلٍ فَٰكِهُونَ ﴿٥٥﴾ هُمْ
وَأَزْوَٰجُهُمْ فِى ظِلَٰلٍ عَلَى ٱلْأَرَآئِكِ مُتَّكِـُٔونَ ﴿٥٦﴾ لَهُمْ فِيهَا
فَٰكِهَةٌ وَلَهُم مَّا يَدَّعُونَ ﴿٥٧﴾ سَلَٰمٌ قَوْلًا مِّن رَّبٍّ رَّحِيمٍ ﴿٥٨﴾

[55] Indeed the companions of Paradise shall that Day have joy in all they do. [56] They and their

> spouses, in shade, reclining on thrones. [57] For them therein is fruit and whatever they should call for, [58] (And) 'Peace,' a salutation from a merciful Lord.

The righteous believers, by Allah's mercy, will not wait long for their accounts on the Day of Judgement but will pass on quickly after the announcement of their success to the reward awaiting them. As described in the Qur'an:

فَأَمَّا مَنْ أُوتِيَ كِتَٰبَهُۥ بِيَمِينِهِۦ ﴿٧﴾ فَسَوْفَ يُحَاسَبُ حِسَابًا يَسِيرًا ﴿٨﴾ وَيَنقَلِبُ إِلَىٰٓ أَهْلِهِۦ مَسْرُورًا ﴿٩﴾ ﴿الانشقاق﴾

"As for he who has been given his record in his right hand, he will be judged with an easy reckoning and return to his people in joy." (84:7–9)

They will be continually occupied with pleasures beyond the imagination of man in this worldly life—"that which no eye has seen, no ear has heard and has never occurred to a human heart."[1]

Enjoying a life of ease and free of discomfort, the people of Paradise share their joy with spouses most pleasing to them in the shade of gardens:

وَٱلَّذِينَ ءَامَنُوا۟ وَعَمِلُوا۟ ٱلصَّٰلِحَٰتِ سَنُدْخِلُهُمْ جَنَّٰتٍ تَجْرِى مِن تَحْتِهَا ٱلْأَنْهَٰرُ خَٰلِدِينَ فِيهَآ أَبَدًا ۖ لَّهُمْ فِيهَآ أَزْوَٰجٌ مُّطَهَّرَةٌ ۖ وَنُدْخِلُهُمْ ظِلًّا ظَلِيلًا ﴿٥٧﴾ ﴿النساء﴾

1. Al-Bukhārī, Muslim and others.

"… For them therein are purified spouses, and We will admit them to deepening shade." (4:57)

مُّتَّكِـِٔينَ فِيهَا عَلَى ٱلْأَرَآئِكِ ۖ لَا يَرَوْنَ فِيهَا شَمْسًا وَلَا زَمْهَرِيرًا ﴿١٣﴾ ﴿الإنسان﴾

"Reclining therein on thrones, they will see therein neither (burning) sun nor (freezing) cold." (76:13)

Concerning the fruits of Paradise, Ibn Jarīr has commented that they resemble those of our earth in appearance but are far superior in taste. And Ibn 'Abbās said, "What is in Paradise does not resemble what is (known) in this world except in name." But Allah knows best about this. He says:

وَبَشِّرِ ٱلَّذِينَ ءَامَنُواْ وَعَمِلُواْ ٱلصَّـٰلِحَـٰتِ أَنَّ لَهُمْ جَنَّـٰتٍ تَجْرِى مِن تَحْتِهَا ٱلْأَنْهَـٰرُ ۖ كُلَّمَا رُزِقُواْ مِنْهَا مِن ثَمَرَةٍ رِّزْقًا ۙ قَالُواْ هَـٰذَا ٱلَّذِى رُزِقْنَا مِن قَبْلُ ۖ وَأُتُواْ بِهِۦ مُتَشَـٰبِهًا ۖ وَلَهُمْ فِيهَآ أَزْوَٰجٌ مُّطَهَّرَةٌ ۖ وَهُمْ فِيهَا خَـٰلِدُونَ ﴿٢٥﴾ ﴿البقرة﴾

"… Whenever they are provided with a provision of fruit therefrom, they say, 'This is what we were provided with before.' And it is given to them in likeness …" (2:25)

Yet the provisions with which the righteous are rewarded are not limited to fruits but certainly include whatever the soul desires and more:

نَحْنُ أَوْلِيَآؤُكُمْ فِى ٱلْحَيَوٰةِ ٱلدُّنْيَا وَفِى ٱلْـَٔاخِرَةِ ۖ وَلَكُمْ فِيهَا مَا تَشْتَهِىٓ أَنفُسُكُمْ وَلَكُمْ فِيهَا مَا تَدَّعُونَ ﴿٣١﴾ ﴿فصلت﴾

"… And for you therein is whatever your souls long for, and for you therein is whatever you call for." (41:31)

مَنْ عَمِلَ سَيِّئَةً فَلَا يُجْزَىٰٓ إِلَّا مِثْلَهَا ۖ وَمَنْ عَمِلَ صَـٰلِحًا مِّن ذَكَرٍ أَوْ أُنثَىٰ وَهُوَ مُؤْمِنٌ فَأُو۟لَـٰٓئِكَ يَدْخُلُونَ ٱلْجَنَّةَ يُرْزَقُونَ فِيهَا بِغَيْرِ حِسَابٍ ﴿٤٠﴾ ﴿غافر﴾

"… Those will enter Paradise, being given provision therein without measure." (40:40)

In addition to their pleasures, the righteous will be comforted by the word of peace from Allah (ﷻ). And Ibn 'Abbās pointed out that Allah Himself is peace upon the people of Paradise. This *āyah* is similar in meaning to another in which Allah promises:

تَحِيَّتُهُمْ يَوْمَ يَلْقَوْنَهُۥ سَلَـٰمٌ ۚ وَأَعَدَّ لَهُمْ أَجْرًا كَرِيمًا ﴿٤٤﴾ ﴿الأحزاب﴾

"Their greeting the day they meet Him will be 'Peace' …" (33:44)

What could be more desired by the believing soul after its long struggle upon the earth against tyranny, greed and malice than peace—relief from harm and from pain and from animosity—refuge in the eternal peace of Allah (ﷻ).

Āyah 59

وَٱمْتَـٰزُوا۟ ٱلْيَوْمَ أَيُّهَا ٱلْمُجْرِمُونَ ﴿٥٩﴾

[59] But stand apart today, you criminals.

The people of Paradise have passed on to their home of

eternal peace and happiness after a brief and easy reckoning. Now attention is turned to the evildoers, who are told to separate and remove themselves from the ranks of the believers, making their shameful position clear to all; and depriving them of any benefit that they might have hoped for had they remained in the company of those covered by the mercy of Allah. It has been suggested further by some scholars that the criminals are told to separate from each other into the heretical sects and parties to which they had belonged in the world and to be identified with them. As Allah says:

وَيَوْمَ تَقُومُ ٱلسَّاعَةُ يَوْمَئِذٍ يَتَفَرَّقُونَ ﴿١٤﴾ ﴿الرُّوم﴾

"And the day the Hour is established—on that Day they will separate." (30:14)

In other words, they will disperse, divide and be differentiated from one another. Moreover, they will be separated from those they had once followed, worshipped or obeyed other than Allah:

وَيَوْمَ نَحْشُرُهُمْ جَمِيعًا ثُمَّ نَقُولُ لِلَّذِينَ أَشْرَكُوا۟ مَكَانَكُمْ أَنتُمْ وَشُرَكَآؤُكُمْ ۚ
فَزَيَّلْنَا بَيْنَهُمْ ۖ وَقَالَ شُرَكَآؤُهُم مَّا كُنتُمْ إِيَّانَا تَعْبُدُونَ ﴿٢٨﴾ ﴿يُونُس﴾

"One day We shall gather them all together, then We will say to those who associated (others with Allah), 'Stay in your place, you and those you associated.' And We will disperse them …" (10:28)

Isolated and helpless, they await the dreaded account of their misdeeds.

Āyahs 60–61

أَلَمْ أَعْهَدْ إِلَيْكُمْ يَٰبَنِىٓ ءَادَمَ أَن لَّا تَعْبُدُوا۟ ٱلشَّيْطَٰنَ ۖ إِنَّهُۥ
لَكُمْ عَدُوٌّ مُّبِينٌ ﴿٦٠﴾ وَأَنِ ٱعْبُدُونِى ۚ هَٰذَا صِرَٰطٌ مُّسْتَقِيمٌ ﴿٦١﴾

[60] "Did I not enjoin upon you, O children of Adam, that you should not worship Shayṭān, for certainly he is to you a manifest enemy" [61] "And (that you) worship Me? This is a straight path."

The evildoers are brought forward to face the displeasure and anger of Allah, Lord of the Worlds. Having rejected His warning and guidance, preferring instead those unlawful ways once made to seem pleasing by Shayṭān, they are now severely reproached for their foolishness in disobeying the Almighty Creator. Addressing them as "children of Adam," Allah alludes not only to the well-known treachery of Shayṭān in tempting and deceiving their first ancestor and his mate but also to His warning to them:

يَٰبَنِىٓ ءَادَمَ لَا يَفْتِنَنَّكُمُ ٱلشَّيْطَٰنُ كَمَآ أَخْرَجَ أَبَوَيْكُم مِّنَ ٱلْجَنَّةِ يَنزِعُ
عَنْهُمَا لِبَاسَهُمَا لِيُرِيَهُمَا سَوْءَٰتِهِمَآ ۗ إِنَّهُۥ يَرَىٰكُمْ هُوَ وَقَبِيلُهُۥ مِنْ حَيْثُ لَا
تَرَوْنَهُمْ ۗ إِنَّا جَعَلْنَا ٱلشَّيَٰطِينَ أَوْلِيَآءَ لِلَّذِينَ لَا يُؤْمِنُونَ ﴿٢٧﴾ ﴿الأعراف﴾

"O children of Adam, do not let Shayṭān seduce you as he removed your Parents from the Garden …" (7:27)

إِنَّ ٱلشَّيْطَٰنَ لَكُمْ عَدُوٌّ فَٱتَّخِذُوهُ عَدُوًّا ۚ إِنَّمَا يَدْعُوا۟ حِزْبَهُۥ
لِيَكُونُوا۟ مِنْ أَصْحَٰبِ ٱلسَّعِيرِ ﴿٦﴾ ﴿فاطر﴾

"Certainly Shayṭān is an enemy to you, so take him as an enemy …" (35:6)

They had carelessly disregarded the open declaration of war on mankind by Shayṭān who, disdaining righteousness and mercy, had defiantly vowed to lead to destruction any and all who would follow him in disobedience to Allah.

All commentators have stated with certainty that worship of Shayṭān means obeying him in disobedience to al-Raḥmān. The Qur'an declares in the words of Prophet Yūsuf:

مَا تَعْبُدُونَ مِن دُونِهِۦٓ إِلَّآ أَسْمَآءً سَمَّيْتُمُوهَآ أَنتُمْ وَءَابَآؤُكُم مَّآ أَنزَلَ ٱللَّهُ بِهَا مِن سُلْطَٰنٍ ۚ إِنِ ٱلْحُكْمُ إِلَّا لِلَّهِ ۚ أَمَرَ أَلَّا تَعْبُدُوٓا۟ إِلَّآ إِيَّاهُ ۚ ذَٰلِكَ ٱلدِّينُ ٱلْقَيِّمُ وَلَٰكِنَّ أَكْثَرَ ٱلنَّاسِ لَا يَعْلَمُونَ ﴿٤٠﴾ ﴿يوسف﴾

"… Legislation is only for Allah. He has commanded that you not to worship any but Him …" (12:40)

The true, comprehensive definition of "worship" is "submission and obedience". There should be no obedience to any created being that involves disobedience to the Creator, yet Shayṭān invites mankind to oppose divine legislation. Obedience to his agents, is the worship of Shayṭān, just as obedience to those authorities upholding the law of Allah is worship of Him. Those guilty ones who now stand humbled and humiliated in the Hereafter preferred to follow their own desires or those of other men in opposition to divine law and thus became worshippers of Shayṭān.

Had the transgressors accepted truth and returned to Allah in repentance, He would have covered them with His mercy and protected them from their enemy. For He has reassured man that it is within his power to avoid seduction by Shayṭān:

إِنَّهُۥ لَيْسَ لَهُۥ سُلْطَٰنٌ عَلَى ٱلَّذِينَ ءَامَنُوا۟ وَعَلَىٰ رَبِّهِمْ يَتَوَكَّلُونَ ﴿٩٩﴾ إِنَّمَا سُلْطَٰنُهُۥ عَلَى ٱلَّذِينَ يَتَوَلَّوْنَهُۥ وَٱلَّذِينَ هُم بِهِۦ مُشْرِكُونَ ﴿١٠٠﴾ ﴿النحل﴾

"Indeed there is no authority for him (*ie.,* Shayṭān) over those who believe and trust in their Lord. His authority is only over those who turn to him (in obedience) and those who, through him, worship others (than Allah)." (16:99–100)

Among scholars' general definitions of "the straight path" is that taken from this *āyah*, *ie.,* the worship of Allah. In the Qur'an, He has informed us of the purpose for which man was created:

وَمَا خَلَقْتُ ٱلْجِنَّ وَٱلْإِنسَ إِلَّا لِيَعْبُدُونِ ﴿٥٦﴾ ﴿الذاريات﴾

"And I did not create the jinn and mankind except to worship Me." (51:56)

In Islam, worship (*'ibādah*) is not limited to prayer, fasting, *zakāh* and *ḥajj.* It is impossible that the ultimate purpose of man's creation could be realized through acts which require only a small portion of his time and resources. If the remainder of one's existence outside of these four "pillars" is not worship, then life surely falls short of the purpose stated by Allah (ﷻ). On the other hand, it is beyond the ability of man to spend his entire existence in formal rites of worship or in continuous praise of Allah throughout the day and night, as do the angels. Therefore, logically as well as linguistically, the concept of worship must include all of a servant's motivations and actions throughout his lifetime. Additionally, Allah states in the Qur'an that He created man in order to test him,[2] and this trial entails how completely he will fulfill the purpose for which he was created. He commands:

إِنَّ هَٰذِهِۦٓ أُمَّتُكُمۡ أُمَّةٗ وَٰحِدَةٗ وَأَنَا۠ رَبُّكُمۡ فَٱعۡبُدُونِ ﴿٩٢﴾ ﴿الأنبياء﴾

"This, your community, is one community, and I am your Lord so worship Me" (21:92), meaning obedience and striving through *tawḥīd,* for the acceptance and pleasure of Allah.

"This is a straight path" leading directly to Him for those who so desire. As Allah (ﷻ) states in another *āyah*:

وَأَنَّ هَٰذَا صِرَٰطِي مُسۡتَقِيمٗا فَٱتَّبِعُوهُۖ وَلَا تَتَّبِعُواْ ٱلسُّبُلَ فَتَفَرَّقَ بِكُمۡ
عَن سَبِيلِهِۦۚ ذَٰلِكُمۡ وَصَّىٰكُم بِهِۦ لَعَلَّكُمۡ تَتَّقُونَ ﴿١٥٣﴾ ﴿الأنعام﴾

"And this is My path, which is straight, so follow it. And do not follow (other) ways so that you would be separated from My way …" (6:153) And He warns:

وَإِن تُطِعۡ أَكۡثَرَ مَن فِي ٱلۡأَرۡضِ يُضِلُّوكَ عَن سَبِيلِ ٱللَّهِۚ إِن
يَتَّبِعُونَ إِلَّا ٱلظَّنَّ وَإِنۡ هُمۡ إِلَّا يَخۡرُصُونَ ﴿١١٦﴾ ﴿الأنعام﴾

---

2. 18:7; 67:2 and 76:2.

"If you obey most of those upon the earth, they will lead you astray from the way of Allah ..." (6:116)

Āyah 62

وَلَقَدْ أَضَلَّ مِنكُمْ جِبِلًّا كَثِيرًا ۖ أَفَلَمْ تَكُونُوا۟ تَعْقِلُونَ ﴿٦٢﴾

[62] "And he had (already) led astray from among you much of creation, so did you not have intelligence?"

Allah (ﷻ) continues His reproach of the criminals by reminding them of their failure to benefit from the experience of past generations. History abounds with examples of societies and nations that fell prey to Shayṭān and thus met with destruction, defeat and dishonor in this world even before the Next. Are these examples not sufficient to dissuade those of intelligence and perception from repeating the same errors? Many such stories are related in the Qur'an for that very purpose, yet how many Muslims have actually opened their eyes and availed themselves of the lessons contained in them?

۞ أَفَلَمْ يَسِيرُوا۟ فِى ٱلْأَرْضِ فَيَنظُرُوا۟ كَيْفَ كَانَ عَـٰقِبَةُ ٱلَّذِينَ مِن قَبْلِهِمْ ۚ دَمَّرَ ٱللَّهُ عَلَيْهِمْ ۖ وَلِلْكَـٰفِرِينَ أَمْثَـٰلُهَا ﴿١٠﴾ ﴿محمد﴾

"Did they not proceed throughout the earth and observe how was the end of those before them?..."[3]

3. 47:10; 30:9; 35:44; 12:109; 22:46; 40:21 and 40:82 contain the same meaning with a slight difference in wording.

Allah encourages believers of every generation to observe and contemplate:

قُلْ سِيرُوا۟ فِى ٱلْأَرْضِ ثُمَّ ٱنظُرُوا۟ كَيْفَ كَانَ عَـٰقِبَةُ ٱلْمُكَذِّبِينَ ﴿١١﴾ ﴿الأنعام﴾

"So travel through the earth and observe how was the end of those who denied."[4]

Today one can move about the earth from his own home—through a film, broadcast, book or newspaper—gaining information about every people and every event, past and present. Is not the handiwork of Shayṭān obvious to all?

Āyah 63

هَـٰذِهِۦ جَهَنَّمُ ٱلَّتِى كُنتُمْ تُوعَدُونَ ﴿٦٣﴾

[63] "This is the Hellfire which you were promised."

The Hellfire is now brought before the condemned, just as Allah States:

وَعَرَضْنَا جَهَنَّمَ يَوْمَئِذٍ لِّلْكَـٰفِرِينَ عَرْضًا ﴿١٠٠﴾ ﴿الكهف﴾

"And We present the Hellfire that Day on display before the disbelievers." (18:100)

Ibn Kathīr has pointed out that here Allah indicates that He will show them the Hellfire to let them see what it contains of retribution and punishment before their entry into it. The horror of anticipation allows for even deeper regret and additional anguish.

---

4. 3:137 and 16:36. In 6:11; 27:69 and 30:42, the Prophet (ﷺ) is ordered to say: "Travel through the earth and observe ...".

It is related by Ibn Mas'ūd that the Prophet (ﷺ) said, "The Hellfire will be brought, being led from seventy thousand halters—at each one, seventy thousand angels pulling it"[5]

And Abū Hurayrah reported that he said, "The fire of Hell was burned for a thousand years until it became red. Then it was burned for a thousand years until it became white. Then it was burned for a thousand years until it became black. It is now extremely black."[6]

Āyah 64

ٱصۡلَوۡهَا ٱلۡيَوۡمَ بِمَا كُنتُمۡ تَكۡفُرُونَ ﴿٦٤﴾

[64] Burn therein today for what you used to deny.

The sentence is announced. The punishment is before them. They are powerless to resist the command, "Enter it and burn!" which is accompanied by a reminder that what is impending is none but recompense for what they themselves had earned, as their denial of Allah had opened for them the door to every sin.

The position of those condemned to the Hellfire is further described in Sūrah al-An'ām:

وَلَوۡ تَرَىٰٓ إِذۡ وُقِفُواْ عَلَى ٱلنَّارِ فَقَالُواْ يَٰلَيۡتَنَا نُرَدُّ وَلَا نُكَذِّبَ
بِـَٔايَٰتِ رَبِّنَا وَنَكُونَ مِنَ ٱلۡمُؤۡمِنِينَ ﴿٢٧﴾ بَلۡ بَدَا لَهُم مَّا كَانُواْ يُخۡفُونَ
مِن قَبۡلُۖ وَلَوۡ رُدُّواْ لَعَادُواْ لِمَا نُهُواْ عَنۡهُ وَإِنَّهُمۡ لَكَٰذِبُونَ ﴿٢٨﴾ ﴿الأنعام﴾

5. Muslim.
6. Al-Tirmidhī.

"If you could but see when they are made to stand before the Fire and they say, 'If only we could be returned (to life on earth) and not deny the signs of our Lord and be among the believers.' But that which they concealed has (now) appeared to them, and if they were returned, they would indeed return to that which they were forbidden. And certainly they are liars." (6:27–28)

Āyah 65

ٱلْيَوْمَ نَخْتِمُ عَلَىٰٓ أَفْوَٰهِهِمْ وَتُكَلِّمُنَآ أَيْدِيهِمْ وَتَشْهَدُ أَرْجُلُهُم بِمَا كَانُوا۟ يَكْسِبُونَ ﴿٦٥﴾

> [65] That day We will seal up their mouths, and their hands will speak to Us, and their feet will testify about what they used to earn.

The rejecters (of faith) and the hypocrites, who pretended faith, will try to escape punishment by denying their crimes. They will attempt to defend themselves with lies and false oaths as was their habit during earthly life.[7] But Allah will seal their mouths, silencing untruth, and cause their limbs to speak about all that they had done.

Concerning the silencing of the disbelievers, Anas bin Mālik reported, "We were with the Messenger of Allah (ﷺ), and he smiled so much that his molars appeared. Then he said, 'Do you know what I am laughing at?' We said, 'Allah and His Messenger know most.' He said, 'At a

7. As described in 58:18.

servant's discussion with his Lord, he will say, "O Lord, will You not protect me from injustice?" And Allah (ﷻ) will say, "Yes". So he will declare, "Then I shall not accept any witness against me except one from myself" At that, He will say, "Sufficient as a witness against you today is yourself, and as witnesses, the honorable recording angels." And his mouth will be sealed, and it will be said to the parts of his body, "Speak," and they will speak of his deeds. Then he will be allowed to talk (once again), and he will say (to his limbs), "Away with you! For it was on your behalf that I was disputing."[8]

Thus the evil ones find that their own bodies betray them on the Day of Judgement and oppose them with the truth. In Sūrah Fuṣṣilat it is further stated that their hearing, sight and skins will witness against the enemies of Allah.[9]

وَقَالُوا۟ لِجُلُودِهِمْ لِمَ شَهِدتُّمْ عَلَيْنَا ۖ قَالُوٓا۟ أَنطَقَنَا ٱللَّهُ ٱلَّذِىٓ أَنطَقَ كُلَّ شَىْءٍ وَهُوَ خَلَقَكُمْ أَوَّلَ مَرَّةٍ وَإِلَيْهِ تُرْجَعُونَ ﴿٢١﴾ ﴿فصلت﴾

"And they will say to their skins, 'Why did you testify against us?' They will say (in reply), 'We were made to speak by Allah, Who has made everything speak, and it is He Who created you and to Him you are returned.'" (41:21)

The senses and body members, which were once under the servant's control and were misused during earthly life,

---

8. Muslim and al-Nasā'ī.
9. See 41:19–20.

are no longer subject to him but only to the justice of Allah. Ibn 'Abbās said, "On the Day of Judgement there will come upon the people a time when they will not speak or make an excuse or utter a word until permission is granted them. Then they will dispute their judgement, and one who associated partners with Allah will deny that he associated, and the people will swear to Him as they (now) swear to you. But while they are denying (their crimes), Allah will call forth witnesses from themselves—their skins, their sight, their hands and their feet, and He will seal their mouths. Then He will open mouths in the body parts, and they (*ie.,* the body parts) will argue. They will say, 'We were made to speak by Allah, Who has made everything speak ...' And so the tongues will be conquered after their denial."

It is also reported by Abū Mūsā al-Ash'ārī that the disbelievers and hypocrites will say, "This angel has recorded that which I did not do." The angel will inquire, "Did you not do this and that on such and such day?" He will declare, "No, by Your power, O Lord, I did not do it." Thereupon, Allah will seal his mouth.

If the scene portrayed in this *āyah* seems strange or inconceivable, it is, in reality, but one of the endless possibilities and alternatives to the creation which is familiar to us on the earth. The potentialities of the Hereafter far exceeding those of the present universe, nothing is beyond the all-powerful, all-capable Creator.

The verses in Sūrah Fuṣṣilat conclude:

وَمَا كُنتُمْ تَسْتَتِرُونَ أَن يَشْهَدَ عَلَيْكُمْ سَمْعُكُمْ وَلَآ أَبْصَـٰرُكُمْ وَلَا جُلُودُكُمْ وَلَـٰكِن ظَنَنتُمْ أَنَّ ٱللَّهَ لَا يَعْلَمُ كَثِيرًا مِّمَّا تَعْمَلُونَ ﴿٢٢﴾ وَذَٰلِكُمْ ظَنُّكُمُ ٱلَّذِى ظَنَنتُم بِرَبِّكُمْ أَرْدَىٰكُمْ فَأَصْبَحْتُم مِّنَ ٱلْخَـٰسِرِينَ ﴿٢٣﴾ ﴿فُصِّلَتْ﴾

"And you were not protecting yourselves (with piety), lest your hearing witness against you or your sight or your skins, but you supposed that Allah does not know much of what you do. And that was your supposition which you supposed about your Lord. It has brought you to ruin, and you have become among those who have lost completely." (41:22–23)

Āyah 66

وَلَوْ نَشَآءُ لَطَمَسْنَا عَلَىٰٓ أَعْيُنِهِمْ فَٱسْتَبَقُوا۟ ٱلصِّرَٰطَ فَأَنَّىٰ يُبْصِرُونَ ﴿٦٦﴾

> [66] Yet if We willed, We could have done away with their eyes, and they would race to reach the path, but how could they see?

Among the blessings usually taken for granted by man are two vital capabilities without which he would be reduced to helplessness—those of vision and movement. In human existence these facilities are meant to serve a higher purpose than they do in animals. Allah (ﷻ) has provided through them the ability to perceive the truth and to act upon it during one's lifetime on earth. Refusal to employ them in the responsible manner befitting humanity leads to two grave consequences: the loss of these abilities even during earthly life, as described in *āyah* 9, and humiliation and punishment in the Hereafter, as revealed in *āyahs* 59–65. Allah (ﷻ) points out that He could just as easily have left man without a means to guidance or to the pursuit of righteousness. How miserable, then, would his condition have been.

The use of the verb *ṭamasa* (طَمَسَ) specifies not only that Allah could have blinded them but that He could have completely wiped out any trace of their eyes. Ibn 'Abbās added, "He could have prevented them from guidance or from seeing the path of truth." But al-Raḥmān, the All-Merciful, did not leave His servants to grope blindly; rather, He gave them every opportunity to benefit themselves in this world and the Next.

Āyah 67

وَلَوْ نَشَآءُ لَمَسَخْنَٰهُمْ عَلَىٰ مَكَانَتِهِمْ فَمَا ٱسْتَطَٰعُوا۟
مُضِيًّا وَلَا يَرْجِعُونَ ﴿٦٧﴾

> [67] And if We willed, We could have deformed them (paralyzing them) in their places so they would neither be able to move on, nor could they return.

Freedom of movement is a blessing which enables man to realize many objectives throughout life and to work for eternal happiness in the Hereafter. But if He had willed, Allah (ﷻ) could have deprived him of this capability as well.

Masakha (مَسَخ) carries the meaning of "petrification, transformation into a solid state or into an inferior kind of being or beast." Scholars have explained the *āyah,* saying that Allah (ﷻ) could have destroyed the criminals in their homes or in the place where they were committing sins, or He could have paralyzed their legs or turned them into stone. Yet He did not do so. Instead He gave them additional chances and occasions to repent and return to His grace.

The scenes of helplessness portrayed in this and the previous *āyah* are a reminder to all men of their ultimate dependence upon Allah's favor. For as long as the body continues to function well, man is proud and confident. But once his abilities are impaired, he is forced to face the reality of his own limitations. Surely there will come a day when all human power and freedom must be relinquished to Him Who granted it for a time.

Āyah 68

وَمَن نُّعَمِّرْهُ نُنَكِّسْهُ فِي ٱلْخَلْقِ ۖ أَفَلَا يَعْقِلُونَ ﴿٦٨﴾

[68] And he to whom We grant long life We reverse in creation; so will they not understand?

Allah (ﷻ) has already depicted the limitations of humankind in two ways—the complete loss of control over one's affairs after death and in the Hereafter, and the possibility of incapacity during worldly life. A third limitation is mentioned here—the waning of physical and mental powers in old age. As much as man has sought to prevent it, inevitable decline and deterioration sets in visibly upon those far advanced in years. The Prophet (ﷺ) said, "Use medication, O servants of Allah. For Allah did not make an ailment but that He made a cure for it, except for one ailment—old age."[10]

The Qur'an makes further references to the same fact:

وَٱللَّهُ خَلَقَكُمْ ثُمَّ يَتَوَفَّىٰكُمْ ۚ وَمِنكُم مَّن يُرَدُّ إِلَىٰٓ أَرْذَلِ ٱلْعُمُرِ لِكَىْ لَا يَعْلَمَ بَعْدَ عِلْمٍ شَيْـًٔا ۚ إِنَّ ٱللَّهَ عَلِيمٌ قَدِيرٌ ﴿٧٠﴾ ﴿النحل﴾

"And among you is he who is returned to the most decrepit (old) age so that he knows nothing after (he once had) knowledge …"[11] And the reversal in creation is also described thus:

۞ ٱللَّهُ ٱلَّذِى خَلَقَكُم مِّن ضَعْفٍ ثُمَّ جَعَلَ مِنۢ بَعْدِ ضَعْفٍ قُوَّةً ثُمَّ جَعَلَ مِنۢ بَعْدِ قُوَّةٍ ضَعْفًا وَشَيْبَةً ۚ يَخْلُقُ مَا يَشَآءُ ۖ وَهُوَ ٱلْعَلِيمُ ٱلْقَدِيرُ ﴿٥٤﴾ ﴿الروم﴾

"It is Allah Who created you in weakness; then He made after weakness strength; then He made after strength weakness and white hair ..." (30:54)

Reversal is evident in the emergence of weakness after strength. The aged person is in need of care and assistance to manage his affairs, as is a child before maturity. Mental

---

10. Al-Bukhārī, Aḥmad and al-Tirmidhī.
11. 16:70 and 22:5.

function is often impaired, and emotions surface. Senility in many ways resembles the state of early childhood. Reversal is evident as well in the physical appearance of the extremely aged and in his resemblance to the unborn fetus. For Allah created man originally from the elements of the earth and then brought him into the world through his mother's womb. One who completes a maximum life span shows the natural signs of reversal, for soon he will return to the earth, from which he came—to disintegrate and become of its elements once again, his soul awaiting the second creation as it once awaited the first.

The Prophet (ﷺ) used to supplicate, "O Allah, I seek refuge in You from laziness and from cowardice, from decrepitude and from stinginess"[12] and "I seek refuge in You from being returned to the most decrepit old age."[13]

Ibn Kathīr has commented about the state of this world—that it is a temporary home of transition and cessation, not a home of stability and eternity. "And for this reason," he says, "Allah concludes: '... so will they not understand?'—meaning, will they not use their minds to think about the beginning of their creation and the process of transformation and aging in order to realize that they were created ultimately for another home, which they will never leave or be transported therefrom—the final home of the Hereafter."

---

12. Al-Bukharī, the book of *Du'ā'*:
اللَّهُمَّ إِنِّي أَعُوذُ بِكَ مِنْ الْكَسَلِ وَأَعُوذُ بِكَ مِنْ الْجُبْنِ وَأَعُوذُ بِكَ مِنْ الْهَرَمِ وَأَعُوذُ بِكَ مِنْ الْبُخْلِ

13. Al-Bukhārī, the book of *Du'ā'*:
أَعُوذُ بِكَ مِنْ أَنْ نُرَدَّ إِلَى أَرْذَلِ الْعُمُرِ

ĀYAHS 69–83

وَمَا عَلَّمْنَـٰهُ ٱلشِّعْرَ وَمَا يَنۢبَغِى لَهُۥٓ ۚ إِنْ هُوَ إِلَّا ذِكْرٌ وَقُرْءَانٌ مُّبِينٌ ﴿٦٩﴾
لِّيُنذِرَ مَن كَانَ حَيًّا وَيَحِقَّ ٱلْقَوْلُ عَلَى ٱلْكَـٰفِرِينَ ﴿٧٠﴾ أَوَلَمْ يَرَوْا۟ أَنَّا
خَلَقْنَا لَهُم مِّمَّا عَمِلَتْ أَيْدِينَآ أَنْعَـٰمًا فَهُمْ لَهَا مَـٰلِكُونَ ﴿٧١﴾ وَذَلَّلْنَـٰهَا
لَهُمْ فَمِنْهَا رَكُوبُهُمْ وَمِنْهَا يَأْكُلُونَ ﴿٧٢﴾ وَلَهُمْ فِيهَا مَنَـٰفِعُ وَمَشَارِبُ ۖ أَفَلَا
يَشْكُرُونَ ﴿٧٣﴾ وَٱتَّخَذُوا۟ مِن دُونِ ٱللَّهِ ءَالِهَةً لَّعَلَّهُمْ يُنصَرُونَ ﴿٧٤﴾
لَا يَسْتَطِيعُونَ نَصْرَهُمْ وَهُمْ لَهُمْ جُندٌ مُّحْضَرُونَ ﴿٧٥﴾ فَلَا يَحْزُنكَ
قَوْلُهُمْ ۘ إِنَّا نَعْلَمُ مَا يُسِرُّونَ وَمَا يُعْلِنُونَ ﴿٧٦﴾ أَوَلَمْ يَرَ ٱلْإِنسَـٰنُ أَنَّا
خَلَقْنَـٰهُ مِن نُّطْفَةٍ فَإِذَا هُوَ خَصِيمٌ مُّبِينٌ ﴿٧٧﴾ وَضَرَبَ لَنَا مَثَلًا وَنَسِىَ
خَلْقَهُۥ ۖ قَالَ مَن يُحْىِ ٱلْعِظَـٰمَ وَهِىَ رَمِيمٌ ﴿٧٨﴾ قُلْ يُحْيِيهَا ٱلَّذِىٓ
أَنشَأَهَآ أَوَّلَ مَرَّةٍ ۖ وَهُوَ بِكُلِّ خَلْقٍ عَلِيمٌ ﴿٧٩﴾ ٱلَّذِى جَعَلَ لَكُم مِّنَ
ٱلشَّجَرِ ٱلْأَخْضَرِ نَارًا فَإِذَآ أَنتُم مِّنْهُ تُوقِدُونَ ﴿٨٠﴾ أَوَلَيْسَ ٱلَّذِى خَلَقَ
ٱلسَّمَـٰوَٰتِ وَٱلْأَرْضَ بِقَـٰدِرٍ عَلَىٰٓ أَن يَخْلُقَ مِثْلَهُم ۚ بَلَىٰ وَهُوَ ٱلْخَلَّـٰقُ
ٱلْعَلِيمُ ﴿٨١﴾ إِنَّمَآ أَمْرُهُۥٓ إِذَآ أَرَادَ شَيْـًٔا أَن يَقُولَ لَهُۥ كُن فَيَكُونُ ﴿٨٢﴾
فَسُبْحَـٰنَ ٱلَّذِى بِيَدِهِۦ مَلَكُوتُ كُلِّ شَىْءٍ وَإِلَيْهِ تُرْجَعُونَ ﴿٨٣﴾

[69] And We did not give him knowledge of poetry, nor is it befitting of him. It is none other than a remembrance and a clear Qur'an—[70] To warn whoever is alive and establish the Word against the disbelievers. [71] Do they not see that We have created for them from what Our hands have made, *an'ām*, and then they are their owners? [72] And We have subjected these to them; so some they ride and some they eat. [73] And there are in them (various) benefits and drink. So will they not give thanks? [74] Yet they have taken for themselves gods other than Allah that perhaps they would be helped. [75] They are not able to help them, and, (moreover), they are soldiers in attendance for them. [76] So let not their speech grieve you. Indeed We know what they conceal and what they declare. [77] Does mankind not consider that We created him from a sperm-drop—then he has become an open adversary? [78] He presents an example for Us and forgets his (own) creation. He says, "Who will give life to bones when they are decayed?" [79] Say, "He will give them life—Who produced them the first time—and He is supreme in knowledge of all creation"—[80] The One Who made for you from the green tree, fire, and then you ignite from it. [81] Is not He Who created the heavens and the earth able to create the likes of them? Yes, (it is so). And He is the omniscient Creator. [82] His command when He intends a thing is only that He says to it, "Be" and it is. [83] So praise be to Him in Whose hand is the dominion of all things, and to Him you will be returned.

Āyahs 69–70

وَمَا عَلَّمْنَـٰهُ ٱلشِّعْرَ وَمَا يَنۢبَغِى لَهُۥٓ ۚ إِنْ هُوَ إِلَّا ذِكْرٌ وَقُرْءَانٌ
مُّبِينٌ ﴿٦٩﴾ لِّيُنذِرَ مَن كَانَ حَيًّا وَيَحِقَّ ٱلْقَوْلُ عَلَى
ٱلْكَـٰفِرِينَ ﴿٧٠﴾

> [69] And We did not give him knowledge of poetry nor is it befitting of him. It is none other than a remembrance and a clear Qur'an [70] To warn whoever is alive and establish the Word against the disbelievers.

In this final section, Allah (ﷻ) turns our attention once again to the three main themes of the Sūrah—the prophethood of Muḥammad (ﷺ), creation and its relationship to the Creator, and the Resurrection. The subjects are mentioned briefly by way of review, yet they are presented anew with conclusive statements of evidence based upon reason and reality, which can leave no doubt in the open mind and honest heart.

The first topic dealt with is that with which the Sūrah began—the prophethood of Muḥammad (ﷺ) and the nature of his message. This *āyah* contains a reply to those who claimed that the Prophet was a poet and that the Qur'an was poetry. Those claims of the Qurayshī elite were part of a larger propaganda war launched by them against Islam and its Prophet (ﷺ) in an attempt to discredit him and conceal the true nature of the revelation that was coming to him. The Qur'an documents the protests of the Quraysh:

وَيَقُولُونَ أَئِنَّا لَتَارِكُوٓا۟ ءَالِهَتِنَا لِشَاعِرٍ مَّجْنُونٍۭ ﴿٣٦﴾

"And they say, 'Are we to abandon our gods for a mad poet?'" (37:36)

Far from being unaware of the difference between poetry and the words of the Qur'an, they themselves were masters of poetry and completely familiar with it. Poetry was their art, their skill and their pride. The Qur'an was clearly not in the rhythm or style of poetry, yet they were at a loss to explain the forceful attraction of its verses otherwise without making an admission that would damage their position. In the hope of confusing and distracting the common people, they described it as magic or poetry—the skill of human beings or *jinn*—but nothing more.

Allah directly refutes these allegations in this particular *āyah.* He denies giving the knowledge of poetry to the Prophet, meaning that since He did not provide such knowledge, there was no way at all he could have obtained it. It was reported by those who knew him best, Abū Bakr, 'Umar and 'Ā'ishah (ﷺ), that the Messenger of Allah never memorized poetry, and on occasion when he attempted to quote a verse for some reason, he usually made a mistake in it.[1]

In this *āyah* there is denial not only that the Prophet was a poet but even the possibility that he could be one.

---

1. Ibn Kathīr has added that the few rhyming phrases quoted from the Prophet (ﷺ) on the occasions of al-Khandaq and Ḥunayn were uttered spontaneously without his intending poetry. Furthermore, they are not confirmed as being authentic.

Allah (ﷻ) states that it would not be proper or suitable for His messenger to be one who recited poetry. For if that were the case, some might be able to argue again that the Qur'an was a product of his talent for verse. Another reason given by commentators is the great dissimilarity in the natures of human poetry and divine revelation and their obvious incompatibility. For even in its most civilized forms, poetry can be no more than human ideals and longings. Like any human expression, it has the capacity to serve various purposes, both noble and ignoble. As an art form, its goal is to appeal to human emotion. Yet often, as the Arabs would say, "The sweetest of it is that which is most untruthful." In particular, the Arabic poetry of that period was known for its descriptions of women, idle pastimes and immoral pleasures or for its mockery of others and attacks on their honor with the aim of arousing animosity. Whatever its purpose or potential, poetry has its own method, quite in contrast to that of prophethood.

After negating any connection between His revelation and human poetry, Allah (ﷻ) confirms that these words recited by Prophet Muḥammad (ﷺ) are not but a remembrance[2] and a Qur'an[3] which is clear to all.

The Qur'an has a dual purpose, which is stated directly here. First, it warns every living soul on the face of the earth, but only those whose hearts have life will benefit

---

2. Refer to *āyah* 11.
3. A reference to this final scripture which literally means "a word construction, recital or reading".

from the warning. And second, it serves as evidence by which those who reject belief will be condemned. Again, “the Word” refers to the decree of Allah and His knowledge that a large portion of mankind is destined to be punished in Hell.[4] The justification for this decree and its suitability and necessity will become clear to all, for the Qur’an will be proof of the fact that they were warned, even though they refused to heed the warning. Thus, it is both a mercy and a guidance for the believers and clear evidence against the disbelievers.

In this *āyah*, *kufr* (disbelief or rejection) is placed opposite to life, illustrating its similarity to physical death, where the faculties of hearing, sight and understanding do not function and are of no use at all. Thus, we know that in relation to the Qur’an, there are two kinds of people—those who are alive and respond to it, and those who are dead and do not respond.

Āyah 71

أَوَلَمْ يَرَوْا۟ أَنَّا خَلَقْنَا لَهُم مِّمَّا عَمِلَتْ أَيْدِينَآ أَنْعَـٰمًا فَهُمْ لَهَا مَـٰلِكُونَ ﴿٧١﴾

[71] Do they not see that We have created for them from what Our hands have made, *an ʻām*, and then they are their owners?

Next, Allah (ﷻ) returns to the subject of His creation, which is placed at the disposal of mankind—this time with

4. Refer to *āyah* 7.

an example from animal life. *An'ām* cannot be literally translated as "cattle," but it is used to indicate camels, cows (or oxen), sheep and goats.[5] Or it can refer to camels specifically.

"Do they not see?" Al-Qurṭubī and Ibn Kathīr have explained "sight" here as vision of the heart (*ie.,* "Do they not consider and contemplate and realize?") However, Sayyid Quṭb has chosen the more literal meaning: here is a sign from Allah, visible to all, present before their eyes. These animals are created especially for man—for his benefit and enjoyment yet they are creations from among the countless works of Allah (ﷻ) produced by His hands.

"What is made by the hands of Allah" has been defined by scholars as "that which He created Himself without partner or helper," *ie.,* His own creation. One must refrain from speculation about the nature of His hands and simply believe in all of what Allah has said about Himself as being true in such capacity as is suitable to His absolute and perfect majesty. It is stated in the Qur'an that Allah (ﷻ) has certain attributes such as hearing, sight, mercy, anger, etc. Yet He has disassociated Himself from the limitations of human attributes or human imagination. The correct *'aqīdah* (belief) concerning any descriptions of Allah in the Qur'an and in *ḥadīths* has been summarized thus by Ibn Taymiyyah: "Of the (true) belief in Allah is belief in whatever He has described of Himself in His Book and whatever His Messenger has described of Him—(belief)

5. These are mentioned in 6:143–144.

free from distortion or suspension and free from qualification or comparison."[6]

These animals have been created for man, given to him and made subject to his use by al-Raḥmān. "Ownership" refers to the temporary and partial ownership granted to man by Allah, Who is the actual owner of all things, including man himself. And it refers to the ability of an owner to control his possessions and do with them as he pleases.

Āyah 72

وَذَلَّلْنَـٰهَا لَهُمْ فَمِنْهَا رَكُوبُهُمْ وَمِنْهَا يَأْكُلُونَ ﴿٧٢﴾

> [72] And We have subjected these to them; so some they ride and some they eat.

Many animals have a wild and independent nature, but some have been created with a tame disposition and easily submit to man. They serve various purposes, two of which are mentioned here—transport and food. Other *āyahs* in the Qur'an mention these and other uses:

---

6. Distortion (*taḥrīf*): Applying an allegorical meaning which will inevitably be incorrect since it is not based upon knowledge.
Suspension (*ta'ṭīl*): Desertion of the concept altogether or denial that Allah would have such an attribute or quality.
Qualification (*takyīf*): Attempting to explain how a certain attribute or quality could be, while such knowledge lies only with Allah.
Comparison (*tamthīl*): Supposing that divine attributes resemble those of creation, while Allah says:
"There is nothing like unto Him." (42:11)

ٱللَّهُ ٱلَّذِى جَعَلَ لَكُمُ ٱلْأَنْعَٰمَ لِتَرْكَبُوا۟ مِنْهَا وَمِنْهَا تَأْكُلُونَ ﴿٧٩﴾
وَلَكُمْ فِيهَا مَنَٰفِعُ وَلِتَبْلُغُوا۟ عَلَيْهَا حَاجَةً فِى صُدُورِكُمْ وَعَلَيْهَا
وَعَلَى ٱلْفُلْكِ تُحْمَلُونَ ﴿٨٠﴾ ﴿غَافِر﴾

"It is Allah Who made *an'ām* for you—some for you to ride and some for you to eat—and that you may realize any need which is in your hearts; and upon them and upon ships you are carried." (40:79–80)[7]

Said Qutādah describing the blessing in these animals, "Allah has made them obedient and not of a refusing nature. Even if a small boy came to a camel, he could make it kneel, and if he wished, he could make it stand and drive it along, finding it submissive and willing to be led. In the same way, a train of one hundred or more camels could be led by the child, all following his direction." But if Allah had not so willed, men could not have conquered and tamed such animals. As Sayyid Quṭb has pointed out, even a very small creature such as a fly cannot be forced to submit to man as long as Allah has not created within it the tendency to compliance.

Āyah 73

وَلَهُمْ فِيهَا مَنَٰفِعُ وَمَشَارِبُ ۖ أَفَلَا يَشْكُرُونَ ﴿٧٣﴾

[73] And there are in them (various) benefits and drink. So will they not give thanks?

7. See also 23:21–22.

Ibn Kathīr has mentioned some of the benefits alluded to in this *āyah*: "Camels are ridden, eaten and milked. Heavy burdens are carried by them on long journeys to distant lands. Cattle are eaten and milked and used to plow the earth. Sheep are eaten and milked. The hides, hair and wool of all are put to use ..." Having once been the only means to fulfill basic needs, these animals and their byproducts are still essential to us, and it is difficult to imagine life without them. Meat and milk in particular are as yet indispensable to the well-being of man.

Sūrah al-Naḥl gives a similar description (in *āyahs* five through seven), concluding:

وَٱلْخَيْلَ وَٱلْبِغَالَ وَٱلْحَمِيرَ لِتَرْكَبُوهَا وَزِينَةً ۚ وَيَخْلُقُ مَا لَا تَعْلَمُونَ ﴿٨﴾ ﴿النحل﴾

"... And horses, mules and donkeys for you to ride and for beauty, and He creates that which you do not know" (16:8)

"So will they not give thanks?" If they could only appreciate such favors of which the Qur'an reminds them, they would go on to realize that everything one uses during his lifetime upon earth is available only because of the care and mercy of the Creator. Their hearts would then be filled with gratitude and unceasing praise—the true thankfulness which is not limited to the tongue alone but is proved by obedience to Allah in using His blessings in the manner acceptable to Him. For indeed, misuse of blessings, disobedience and the worship of others are the most shameful forms of ingratitude.

Āyah 74

وَٱتَّخَذُوا مِن دُونِ ٱللَّهِ ءَالِهَةً لَّعَلَّهُمْ يُنصَرُونَ ﴿٧٤﴾

[74] Yet they have taken for themselves gods other than Allah that perhaps they would be helped.

Most men are ungrateful indeed. Turning away from the One Who has provided all the good things they enjoy, they attribute these blessings instead to the favor of certain deities or to other people, to blind fortune or to their own efforts. Acknowledging only immediate gratification, they rarely look beyond the life of this world.

Once there were idols of wood and stone. But those who bowed to them in fact worshipped the authority of custom and tradition—the authority of the tribe, family or society in which they sought security and well-being. *Shirk* (association) is still practiced in every corner of the earth, if not represented by pagan idols, then by numerous other obsessions to which the adherents of non-Islamic culture devote themselves—wealth and status, popular personalities, current ideologies, political parties, personal achievements, etc.

وَمِنَ ٱلنَّاسِ مَن يَتَّخِذُ مِن دُونِ ٱللَّهِ أَندَادًا يُحِبُّونَهُمْ كَحُبِّ ٱللَّهِ ۖ وَٱلَّذِينَ ءَامَنُوٓا۟ أَشَدُّ حُبًّا لِّلَّهِ ۗ وَلَوْ يَرَى ٱلَّذِينَ ظَلَمُوٓا۟ إِذْ يَرَوْنَ ٱلْعَذَابَ أَنَّ ٱلْقُوَّةَ لِلَّهِ جَمِيعًا وَأَنَّ ٱللَّهَ شَدِيدُ ٱلْعَذَابِ ﴿١٦٥﴾ ﴿البقرة﴾

"And among the people are those who take other than Allah as equals (to Him). They love them as they (should) love Allah …" (2:165)

Moreover, *shirk* is represented by the people's belief in and dependence upon these earthly powers rather than upon the power of Allah, even though they might bow to Him superficially in prayer. Association takes many forms and varies with time and place: Allah confirms in the Qur'an:

وَمَا يُؤْمِنُ أَكْثَرُهُم بِٱللَّهِ إِلَّا وَهُم مُّشْرِكُونَ ﴿١٠٦﴾ ﴿يوسف﴾

"And most of them believe not in Allah without associating (others as parteners) with Him." (12:106)

Āyah 75

لَا يَسْتَطِيعُونَ نَصْرَهُمْ وَهُمْ لَهُمْ جُندٌ مُّحْضَرُونَ ﴿٧٥﴾

[75] They are not able to help them, and, (moreover), they are soldiers in attendance for them.

Can dependence upon creation be compared to dependence upon the Creator? Even if Shayṭān should make it seem fruitful for a time on the earth, the worship of false gods can only lead to ruin. Placing trust and hope in them brings disappointment in worldly life and even greater loss in the Hereafter:

أَمْ لَهُمْ ءَالِهَةٌ تَمْنَعُهُم مِّن دُونِنَا ۚ لَا يَسْتَطِيعُونَ نَصْرَ أَنفُسِهِمْ
وَلَا هُم مِّنَّا يُصْحَبُونَ ﴿٤٣﴾ ﴿الأنبياء﴾

"Or have they gods that can guard them from Us? They are not able to help (even) themselves, nor can they be protected from Us." (21:43)

مَثَلُ ٱلَّذِينَ ٱتَّخَذُواْ مِن دُونِ ٱللَّهِ أَوْلِيَآءَ كَمَثَلِ ٱلْعَنكَبُوتِ ٱتَّخَذَتْ بَيْتًا ۖ وَإِنَّ أَوْهَنَ ٱلْبُيُوتِ لَبَيْتُ ٱلْعَنكَبُوتِ ۖ لَوْ كَانُواْ يَعْلَمُونَ ﴿٤١﴾ ﴿العنكبوت﴾

"The example of those who take protectors other than Allah is like that of the spider who takes for itself a home. And truly the weakest of homes is the home of the spider, if they only knew." (29:41)

While Allah (ﷻ) continues eternally to sustain and reign over all creation whether or not His creatures recognize Him, those gods created by men must be maintained and protected by their worshippers in order to exist. If one is amused by the thought of soldiers being posted to protect stone idols from harm in ancient times, he should contemplate the fact that the tyrants and oppressors of our own age who set themselves up as gods to be praised and obeyed without question are just as vulnerable. Their servants must continually stand guard to protect them from those of their people who refuse submission, using all means of propaganda, bribery, threat and persecution to keep their lords in power. Yet can these slaves expect help from their masters when problems arise, or are they merely cast aside as unworthy, insignificant and dispensable after their years of devoted service?

In addition to the aforementioned explanation of this *āyah*, a second interpretation has been given, which is as follows: If any man thinks that he can be helped by lords other than Allah, his trust will betray him on the Day of Judgement. Those he had obeyed and worshipped will be brought forward as soldiers set against him in Hellfire, cursing him and disassociating themselves from him. And Allah knows best.

Āyah 76

فَلَا يَحْزُنكَ قَوْلُهُمْ إِنَّا نَعْلَمُ مَا يُسِرُّونَ وَمَا يُعْلِنُونَ ﴿٧٦﴾

> [76] So let not their speech grieve you. Indeed We know what they conceal and what they declare.

Allah (ﷻ) addresses His messenger with words of comfort and assurance: "Do not be saddened by the campaign of those who waste themselves in the worship of creation, O Muḥammad, against you. And do not be saddened by their denunciation of you as a poet, magician or madman or by their denial of your message to them."

For those who give loyalty to others and refuse gratitude to Allah cannot conceal themselves from His knowledge. He is well aware of their innermost secrets, as well as their public declarations. He knows that deep in their hearts they are not convinced of what they say (as Abū Jahl admitted privately to al-Akhnas bin Shurayq), but they will not relent in their struggle to preserve their own status and authority.

Āyah 77

أَوَلَمْ يَرَ ٱلْإِنسَٰنُ أَنَّا خَلَقْنَٰهُ مِن نُّطْفَةٍ فَإِذَا هُوَ خَصِيمٌ مُّبِينٌ ﴿٧٧﴾

[77] Does mankind not consider that We created him from a sperm-drop—then he has become an open adversary?

The Sūrah concludes with a discussion of Resurrection, the concept most often denied by disbelievers. Evidence is now presented in a final statement which leaves no room for further argument. The circumstance of this revelation was described by several of the *tābi'ūn* as follows: One of the influential leaders of the Quraysh, Ubayy bin Khalaf,[8] came to the Messenger of Allah (ﷺ) with a decayed bone in hand. While crumbling it and scattering it in the wind, he taunted, "O Muḥammad, do you claim that Allah will bring this to life?" He replied, "Yes. Allah will cause you to die, then He will bring you to life, and then He will pack you into the Fire." Immediately thereafter Allah revealed the last *āyahs* of Sūrah Yā Sīn. After quoting this incident Ibn Kathīr has pointed out that the *āyahs* are general in answer to everyone who denies Resurrection, as the word "mankind" (*al-Insān*) indicates.

Elsewhere in the Qur'an, Allah reminds the proud human race of its humble origin:

8. Some said it was al-'Āṣ bin Wā'il. It is possible that more than one person came to the Prophet (ﷺ) with the same objection.

﴿أَلَمْ نَخْلُقكُّم مِّن مَّآءٍ مَّهِينٍ ۝٢٠﴾ ﴿المرسلات﴾

"Did We not create you from a liquid disdained?" (77:20). Upon the creation of Adam from the earth's dust, Allah willed that his descendants would enter the world through the same reproductive process as the basest of animals—a fact which man in his delusion of intellect and self-importance would often prefer to ignore. Yet the reality stands that he evolved from a tiny cell in a drop of fluid belittled in his own estimation. It is related that the Messenger of Allah (ﷺ) one day spat into the palm of his hand and put his finger into it, saying, "Allah says, 'O son of Adam, how can you consider (anything) impossible for Me when I have created you from the likes of this?'"[9]

The process of development from sperm cell to fetus to child to man is in itself a sign of Allah's creative power.[10] With no contrivance on his part, the human being grows physically and mentally until he becomes aware of himself as an individual and of certain characteristics and skills he has been given. But the disbeliever attributes these gifts to himself only and considers that he is self-sufficient. When reminded of his true position as a servant of Allah, his pride will not allow him to reconsider. Upon being warned of the Account and Judgement in a life to come, his reaction is denial and rejection. He becomes an open adversary to those who warn him and ultimately to Allah Himself. The

9. Portion of a ḥadīth narrated by Aḥmad and Ibn Mājah.
10. See Sayyid Quṭb's *tafsīr* of Sūrah al-Ṭāriq, (86:8), *In the Shade of the Qur'ān,* vol. 30, for an excellent description.

Qur'an omits the time factor in this *āyah,* showing clearly the absurdity of a creature who, emerging from a lowly drop of semen, has the audacity to stand up in antagonism against his all-powerful Creator.

Āyah 78

وَضَرَبَ لَنَا مَثَلًا وَنَسِيَ خَلْقَهُۥ ۖ قَالَ مَن يُحْيِ ٱلْعِظَـٰمَ وَهِىَ رَمِيمٌ ﴿٧٨﴾

> [75] He presents an example for Us and forgets his (own) creation. He says, "Who will give life to bones when they are decayed?

"The son of Adam insults Me and he should not insult Me, and he denies Me and he should not deny Me. His insult is his saying that I have a son. As for his denial of Me, it is when he says, 'He will not recreate me as He originated me.'" This statement of Allah (ﷻ) is recorded in a *ḥadīth qudsī.*[11] Unable to imagine anything beyond human power or beyond the reach of their own senses, the arrogant and short-sighted, in scoffing at the concept of Resurrection, compare the Creator to creation, with all its limitations. They offer an example by which they think they can prove the finality of death—the last, visible remains of a body disintegrating into dust, soon to disappear completely. Who could ever restore this to life?[12] But they have forgotten

11. Al-Bukhārī.
12. See similar *āyahs*—17:48–49; 23:35–36; 23:82–83; 27:67; 37:16–17; 50:3; 56:47–48 and 79:10–11.

how their own creation began— from dust and then from a single cell. They have forgotten that they were created by a power beyond their own—without their presence or their consent—from nothing.

۞ مَّآ أَشْهَدتُّهُمْ خَلْقَ ٱلسَّمَـٰوَٰتِ وَٱلْأَرْضِ وَلَا خَلْقَ أَنفُسِهِمْ وَمَا كُنتُ مُتَّخِذَ ٱلْمُضِلِّينَ عَضُدًا ﴿٥١﴾ ﴿الكهف﴾

"I did not show them the creation of the heavens and the earth nor the creation of themselves …" (18:51)

Referring directly to the challenge by the Qurayshī chiefs, the Qur'an repeats their expression of ridicule, attracting the attention of all for the answer to come. For the question put to the Prophet (ﷺ), with all its intended sarcasm and insolence, is to serve as a base for the following discourse in which the final evidence is put forth.

Āyahs 79–80

قُلْ يُحْيِيهَا ٱلَّذِىٓ أَنشَأَهَآ أَوَّلَ مَرَّةٍ ۖ وَهُوَ بِكُلِّ خَلْقٍ عَلِيمٌ ﴿٧٩﴾ ٱلَّذِى جَعَلَ لَكُم مِّنَ ٱلشَّجَرِ ٱلْأَخْضَرِ نَارًا فَإِذَآ أَنتُم مِّنْهُ تُوقِدُونَ ﴿٨٠﴾

> [79] Say, "He will give them life—Who produced them the first time—and He is supreme in knowledge of all creation" [80] The One Who made for you from the green tree, fire, and then you ignite from it.

The Prophet (ﷺ) had given an appropriate answer to the

rudeness of Ubayy bin Khalaf and others. But Allah (سبحانه وتعالى) ordered him to give an answer to the doubters and questioners of every age. He commanded him to give the answer obvious to any who would reflect upon the state of the universe—that the bones as a part of the human body will be created and brought to life once more by the same power which created them in the first place from nothing at all. For He Who is able to originate creation at will can certainly renew it at will. This point is also emphasized in other *āyahs:*

وَيَقُولُ ٱلْإِنسَـٰنُ أَءِذَا مَا مِتُّ لَسَوْفَ أُخْرَجُ حَيًّا ﴿٦٦﴾ أَوَلَا
يَذْكُرُ ٱلْإِنسَـٰنُ أَنَّا خَلَقْنَـٰهُ مِن قَبْلُ وَلَمْ يَكُ شَيْـًٔا ﴿٦٧﴾ ﴿مريم﴾

"And man says, 'When I have died, will I indeed be brought forth alive?' Then does man not remember that We created him before, while he was nothing?" (19:66–67)

أَفَعَيِينَا بِٱلْخَلْقِ ٱلْأَوَّلِ ۚ بَلْ هُمْ فِى لَبْسٍ مِّنْ خَلْقٍ جَدِيدٍ ﴿١٥﴾ ﴿ق﴾

"Did We fail in the first creation? Yet they are in doubt of a new creation." (50:15)

أَفَرَءَيْتُم مَّا تُمْنُونَ ﴿٥٨﴾ ءَأَنتُمْ تَخْلُقُونَهُۥٓ أَمْ نَحْنُ ٱلْخَـٰلِقُونَ ﴿٥٩﴾
نَحْنُ قَدَّرْنَا بَيْنَكُمُ ٱلْمَوْتَ وَمَا نَحْنُ بِمَسْبُوقِينَ ﴿٦٠﴾ عَلَىٰٓ أَن نُّبَدِّلَ
أَمْثَـٰلَكُمْ وَنُنشِئَكُمْ فِى مَا لَا تَعْلَمُونَ ﴿٦١﴾ وَلَقَدْ عَلِمْتُمُ ٱلنَّشْأَةَ
ٱلْأُولَىٰ فَلَوْلَا تَذَكَّرُونَ ﴿٦٢﴾ ﴿الواقعة﴾

"Do you see that which you ejaculate? Is it you who creates it, or are We the Creator? We have decreed death among you, and We are not to be defeated in that We shall change your kind and create you in that which you do not know. And you have already known the first creation, so will you not remember?" (56:58–62)[13]

In Sūrah al-'Ankabūt Allah tells His Messenger (ﷺ) to direct man towards the observation and study that will lead him to this very conclusion:

قُلْ سِيرُوا۟ فِى ٱلْأَرْضِ فَٱنظُرُوا۟ كَيْفَ بَدَأَ ٱلْخَلْقَ ۚ ثُمَّ ٱللَّهُ يُنشِئُ
ٱلنَّشْأَةَ ٱلْـَٔاخِرَةَ ۚ إِنَّ ٱللَّهَ عَلَىٰ كُلِّ شَىْءٍ قَدِيرٌ ﴿٢٠﴾ ﴿العنكبوت﴾

"Say, 'Travel through the earth and observe how He began creation. Then Allah will bring up the final creation …'" (29:20)

Man is a product of the earth.[14] His close association with it in life and death provides him with ample opportunities for examination and contemplation. He is invited to look into the beginnings of life upon the earth—plant, animal and human—in every place and from every angle, for here before him are visible examples of the continuing creative process.

---

13. An alternative meaning has been given for *āyah* 61: "That We shall replace the likes of you (with others upon the earth) and create you (in the Hereafter) in that which you do not know."

14. As shown in 7:25; 20:55 and similar *āyahs,* such as Sūrah Nūḥ, (71:17–18), which states:

وَٱللَّهُ أَنۢبَتَكُم مِّنَ ٱلْأَرْضِ نَبَاتًا ﴿١٧﴾ ثُمَّ يُعِيدُكُمْ فِيهَا وَيُخْرِجُكُمْ إِخْرَاجًا ﴿١٨﴾ ﴿نوح﴾

"And Allah has caused you to grow as growth from the earth, and afterwards He makes you return thereto, and He will bring you forth again, a (new) forth-bringing." (71:17–18)

يُخْرِجُ ٱلْحَىَّ مِنَ ٱلْمَيِّتِ وَيُخْرِجُ ٱلْمَيِّتَ مِنَ ٱلْحَىِّ وَيُحْىِ ٱلْأَرْضَ بَعْدَ مَوْتِهَا ۚ وَكَذَٰلِكَ تُخْرَجُونَ ﴿١٩﴾ ﴿الرُّوم﴾

"He brings out the living from the dead, and He brings out the dead from the living; and He gives life to the earth after it was lifeless. And thus will you be brought out." (30:19)[15]

One might look into the birth of an atom or a galaxy as well, for all creation reflects the power of He Who has promised to recreate:

يَوْمَ نَطْوِى ٱلسَّمَآءَ كَطَىِّ ٱلسِّجِلِّ لِلْكُتُبِ ۚ كَمَا بَدَأْنَآ أَوَّلَ خَلْقٍ نُّعِيدُهُۥ ۚ وَعْدًا عَلَيْنَآ ۚ إِنَّا كُنَّا فَٰعِلِينَ ﴿١٠٤﴾ ﴿الأَنْبِيَاء﴾

"... As We began the first creation, We shall repeat it. (That is) a promise binding upon Us. Assuredly We shall carry it out." (21:104)

"And He is supreme in knowledge of all creation." Indeed, Allah (ﷻ) knows its every aspect, its whereabouts, its future, and its final destination.

A specific example is given in this *āyah* to show the unlimited nature of creative power and that realities are not confined to appearances or expectations. To produce an element from its opposite is a greater wonder than that of systematic development, although it is easy for Allah.[16]

The tree could not sprout, grow or remain green without absorbing and retaining large quantities of water, the very

---

15. *ie.,* on the Day of Judgement.
16. Another reference to this phenomenon is found in Sūrah al-Wāqi'ah, (56:71–72).

element which extinguishes fire. Yet fire is produced by the friction of two green twigs against each other—fire which in turn burns green trees. This phenomenon has been explained in recent years by the fact that solar energy is absorbed by leaves, stored in branches and then released upon agitation or ignition. One type of tree known by the desert Arabs was leafless but nonetheless would sometimes ignite itself during a wind. Praise be to Him Who has given all things their particular properties and characteristics!

Āyah 81

أَوَلَيْسَ ٱلَّذِى خَلَقَ ٱلسَّمَـٰوَٰتِ وَٱلْأَرْضَ بِقَـٰدِرٍ عَلَىٰٓ أَن
يَخْلُقَ مِثْلَهُم ۚ بَلَىٰ وَهُوَ ٱلْخَلَّـٰقُ ٱلْعَلِيمُ ﴿٨١﴾

[81] Is not He Who created the heavens and the earth able to create the likes of them? Yes, (it is so). And He is the omniscient Creator.

The creation of the heavens and the earth is so tremendous as to impose failure on human imagination. Within the created universe, processes of formation, transformation, disintegration and reformation constantly occur and reoccur—creation giving way to creation, matter to energy, energy to matter, life to death, death to life. None of this is difficult for Allah, Who poses the question of this verse. Is He not able, after creating all of this from non-existence, to reconstruct the bodies of those souls who await Judgement? As stated in another *āyah*:

أَوَلَمْ يَرَوْا أَنَّ ٱللَّهَ ٱلَّذِى خَلَقَ ٱلسَّمَـٰوَٰتِ وَٱلْأَرْضَ وَلَمْ يَعْىَ بِخَلْقِهِنَّ بِقَـٰدِرٍ عَلَىٰٓ أَن يُحْـِۧىَ ٱلْمَوْتَىٰ ۚ بَلَىٰٓ إِنَّهُۥ عَلَىٰ كُلِّ شَىْءٍ قَدِيرٌ ﴿٣٣﴾ ﴿الأحقاف﴾

"Do they not see that Allah, Who created the heavens and earth and was not incapable of their creation, is able to give life to the dead?..." (46:33)

Commentators have pointed out that all creation is accomplished with equal facility by Allah. However, for the purpose of clarification, a parallel is drawn from human experience. In doing something for the second time, a man is no longer hindered by the same degree of unfamiliarity. Repetition requires less thought and effort on his part; therefore, the task becomes easier for him than it was previously. Allah (ﷻ) alludes to this in the Qur'an:

أَوَلَمْ يَرَوْا۟ كَيْفَ يُبْدِئُ ٱللَّهُ ٱلْخَلْقَ ثُمَّ يُعِيدُهُۥٓ ۚ إِنَّ ذَٰلِكَ عَلَى ٱللَّهِ يَسِيرٌ ﴿١٩﴾ ﴿العنكبوت﴾

"Have they not considered how Allah begins creation (and) then He repeats it? Certainly that is simple for Allah." (29:19)

وَهُوَ ٱلَّذِى يَبْدَؤُا۟ ٱلْخَلْقَ ثُمَّ يُعِيدُهُۥ وَهُوَ أَهْوَنُ عَلَيْهِ ۚ وَلَهُ ٱلْمَثَلُ ٱلْأَعْلَىٰ فِى ٱلسَّمَـٰوَٰتِ وَٱلْأَرْضِ ۚ وَهُوَ ٱلْعَزِيزُ ٱلْحَكِيمُ ﴿٢٧﴾ ﴿الروم﴾

"And it is He Who begins creation, then repeats it, and that is (even) easier for Him ..." (30:27) Origination or repetition—all is easy for Allah. The material of creation is already in existence, merely to be developed at His command. And what is the creation of man in comparison to that of the heavens and the earth and all they contain?[17]

زَعَمَ ٱلَّذِينَ كَفَرُوٓاْ أَن لَّن يُبۡعَثُواْۚ قُلۡ بَلَىٰ وَرَبِّي لَتُبۡعَثُنَّ ثُمَّ لَتُنَبَّؤُنَّ بِمَا عَمِلۡتُمۡۚ وَذَٰلِكَ عَلَى ٱللَّهِ يَسِيرٞ ﴿٧﴾ ﴿التغابن﴾

"The disbelievers claim that they will never be resurrected. Say, 'Yes, (on the contrary), by my Lord. You shall certainly be resurrected; then you will be informed of what you have done. And that is easy for Allah.'" (64:7)

Āyah 82

إِنَّمَآ أَمۡرُهُۥٓ إِذَآ أَرَادَ شَيۡـًٔا أَن يَقُولَ لَهُۥ كُن فَيَكُونُ ﴿٨٢﴾

[82] His command when He intends a thing is only that He says to it, "Be" and it is.

How creation is effected has been expressed by Allah (ﷻ) simply as a direction given by Him in one word: "Be".[18] Reliable scholars have given very little commentary on this and similar *āyahs* in which existence comes about by decree of the Creator, except for the confirmation that when

17. Allah (ﷻ) confirms:

لَخَلۡقُ ٱلسَّمَٰوَٰتِ وَٱلۡأَرۡضِ أَكۡبَرُ مِنۡ خَلۡقِ ٱلنَّاسِ وَلَٰكِنَّ أَكۡثَرَ ٱلنَّاسِ لَا يَعۡلَمُونَ ﴿٥٧﴾ ﴿غافر﴾

"Indeed, the creation of the heavens and the earth is greater than the creation of people, but most of the people know not." (40:57)

18. Belief in Allah's words or speech is again subject to the conditions mentioned by Ibn Taymiyyah. Refer to *āyah* 71.

Allah says to a thing, "Be," then nothing can prevent, oppose or delay its being. As stated in Sūrah al-Qamar:

وَمَآ أَمْرُنَآ إِلَّا وَٰحِدَةٌ كَلَمْحٍۭ بِٱلْبَصَرِ ﴿٥٠﴾ ﴿القمر﴾

"And Our command is but once, like a twinkling of the eye." (54:50) Whether through physical laws of the universe which He has ordained or by miracle outside the normal course of events, the primal cause of all that has been and ever will be is Allah's command. He but says to it, "Be" and it is.

Āyah 83

فَسُبْحَٰنَ ٱلَّذِى بِيَدِهِۦ مَلَكُوتُ كُلِّ شَىْءٍ وَإِلَيْهِ تُرْجَعُونَ ﴿٨٣﴾

> [83] So praise be to Him in Whose hand is the dominion of all things, and to Him you will be returned.

Praise—a suitable closing to a Sūrah which has taken us beyond the limits of time and space, into the human soul, and through various aspects of creation—calling us to witness the signs of Allah. Praise—which is due to Him absolutely, by reason of His attributes of unity and perfection and by reason of the debt of all existence to its Creator. The precise meaning of *subḥāna* is more than "praise," as such. It is a declaration that Allah is far removed from any lack, failing or imperfection that might be attributed to Him by man and free from any equal or associate.

"Dominion" refers to sovereignty and possession, to right and power, to absolute ownership, authority and control over everything in existence, whether visible or invisible. And as is expressed in a similar *āyah*:

تَبَٰرَكَ ٱلَّذِى بِيَدِهِ ٱلْمُلْكُ وَهُوَ عَلَىٰ كُلِّ شَىْءٍ قَدِيرٌ ﴿١﴾ ﴿الملك﴾

"Blessed is He in Whose hand is dominion …" (67:1) All creation is in the hand of Allah—that which has been and that which is yet to be.

Praise, then, is due to Him and Him alone, the Eternal, the Absolute, Who holds destiny in His hand and to Whom every soul shall be returned.

وَٱلْحَمْدُ لِلَّهِ رَبِّ ٱلْعَٰلَمِينَ

REFERENCES

'Abdul-Baqī, M. Fu'ād, *Al-Mu'jam al-Mufahras li Alfāẓ al-Qur'ān*, Cairo: Dār al-Sha'b, 1945.

'Alī, A. Yūsuf, *The Holy Qur'ān* (English commentary), USA: Amānah Corp., revised ed., 1989.

al-'Asqalānī, Ibn Ḥajar, *Fatḥ al-Bārī bi Sharḥ Ṣaḥīḥ al-Bukhārī*, Beirut: Dār al-Ma'rifah, 1390 H.

Harrās, Muḥammad Khalīl, *Sharḥ al-'Aqīdah al-Wāṣiṭiyyah li Shaykh al-Islām Ibn Taymiyyah*, Makkah al-Mukarramah: Mu'assasat Makkah, 5th ed., n.d.

Ibn Daqīq al-'Īd, *Sharḥ al-Arba'īna Ḥadīthan al-Nawawiyyah*, Jeddah: Mu'assasat al-Ṭibā'ati wa al-Ṣaḥāfati wa al-Nashr, 1982.

Ibn Kathīr, Abūl-Fidā' Ismā'īl, *Tafsīr Ibn Kathīr*, Riyāḍ: Maktabat al-Riyāḍ al-Ḥadīthah, 1980.

Ibn Taymiyyah, Aḥmad, *Majmū' Fatāwā Ibn Taymiyyah*, al-Ri'āsah al-'Āmmah li Shu'ūn al-Ḥaramayn al-Sharīfayn, 1404 H.

Lane, E.W., *Arabic English Lexicon*, Cambridge: Islamic Texts Society, 1984.

al-Mawdūdī, Sayyid Abūl-A'lā, *The Meaning of the Qur'ān*, Lahore: Islamic Publications Ltd., 2nd ed., 1978.

al-Nasafī, 'Abdullah bin Aḥmad, *Tafsīr al-Nasafī*, Beirut: Dār al-Kitāb al-'Arabī, 1982.

National Geographic, Washington, D.C., vol. 163, no. 6, June 1983.

al-Nawawī, Muḥyī al-Dīn Yaḥyā, *Ṣaḥīḥ Muslim bi Sharḥ al-Nawawī,* Cairo: Dār al-Rayān li al-Turāth, 1987.

al-Qaṭṭān, Mannā', *Mabāḥith fī 'Ulūm al-Qur'ān*, Riyadh: Mu'assasat al-Risālah, 1982.

al-Qurṭubī, Muḥammad bin Aḥmad, *Al-Jāmi' li Aḥkām al-Qur'ān*, Dār al-Kitāb al-Miṣriyyah, 2nd ed., n.d.

Quṭb, Muḥammad, *Mafāhīm Yanbaghī an Tuṣaḥḥaḥ,* Cairo: Dār al-Shurūq, 1987.

Quṭb, Sayyid, *Fī Ẓilāl al-Qur'ān*, Beirut: Dār al-Shurūq, 1980.

al-Ummah Magazine, vol. 52, Jan. 1985 and vol. 61, Sept. 1985, Doh: Maṭābi' al-Dūḥah al-Ḥadīthah.

يس والقرآن الحكيم

سُورَةُ يسٓ

بِسۡمِ ٱللَّهِ ٱلرَّحۡمَٰنِ ٱلرَّحِيمِ

يسٓ ﴿١﴾ وَٱلۡقُرۡءَانِ ٱلۡحَكِيمِ ﴿٢﴾ إِنَّكَ لَمِنَ ٱلۡمُرۡسَلِينَ ﴿٣﴾
عَلَىٰ صِرَٰطٖ مُّسۡتَقِيمٖ ﴿٤﴾ تَنزِيلَ ٱلۡعَزِيزِ ٱلرَّحِيمِ ﴿٥﴾
لِتُنذِرَ قَوۡمٗا مَّآ أُنذِرَ ءَابَآؤُهُمۡ فَهُمۡ غَٰفِلُونَ ﴿٦﴾ لَقَدۡ
حَقَّ ٱلۡقَوۡلُ عَلَىٰٓ أَكۡثَرِهِمۡ فَهُمۡ لَا يُؤۡمِنُونَ ﴿٧﴾ إِنَّا
جَعَلۡنَا فِيٓ أَعۡنَٰقِهِمۡ أَغۡلَٰلٗا فَهِيَ إِلَى ٱلۡأَذۡقَانِ فَهُم
مُّقۡمَحُونَ ﴿٨﴾ وَجَعَلۡنَا مِنۢ بَيۡنِ أَيۡدِيهِمۡ سَدّٗا وَمِنۡ
خَلۡفِهِمۡ سَدّٗا فَأَغۡشَيۡنَٰهُمۡ فَهُمۡ لَا يُبۡصِرُونَ ﴿٩﴾ وَسَوَآءٌ
عَلَيۡهِمۡ ءَأَنذَرۡتَهُمۡ أَمۡ لَمۡ تُنذِرۡهُمۡ لَا يُؤۡمِنُونَ ﴿١٠﴾ إِنَّمَا
تُنذِرُ مَنِ ٱتَّبَعَ ٱلذِّكۡرَ وَخَشِيَ ٱلرَّحۡمَٰنَ بِٱلۡغَيۡبِۖ فَبَشِّرۡهُ
بِمَغۡفِرَةٖ وَأَجۡرٖ كَرِيمٍ ﴿١١﴾ إِنَّا نَحۡنُ نُحۡيِ ٱلۡمَوۡتَىٰ
وَنَكۡتُبُ مَا قَدَّمُواْ وَءَاثَٰرَهُمۡۚ وَكُلَّ شَيۡءٍ أَحۡصَيۡنَٰهُ فِيٓ
إِمَامٖ مُّبِينٖ ﴿١٢﴾ وَٱضۡرِبۡ لَهُم مَّثَلًا أَصۡحَٰبَ ٱلۡقَرۡيَةِ إِذۡ
جَآءَهَا ٱلۡمُرۡسَلُونَ ﴿١٣﴾ إِذۡ أَرۡسَلۡنَآ إِلَيۡهِمُ ٱثۡنَيۡنِ
فَكَذَّبُوهُمَا فَعَزَّزۡنَا بِثَالِثٖ فَقَالُوٓاْ إِنَّآ إِلَيۡكُم مُّرۡسَلُونَ ﴿١٤﴾

قَالُواْ مَآ أَنتُمۡ إِلَّا بَشَرٞ مِّثۡلُنَا وَمَآ أَنزَلَ ٱلرَّحۡمَٰنُ مِن شَيۡءٍ
إِنۡ أَنتُمۡ إِلَّا تَكۡذِبُونَ ﴿١٥﴾ قَالُواْ رَبُّنَا يَعۡلَمُ إِنَّآ إِلَيۡكُمۡ
لَمُرۡسَلُونَ ﴿١٦﴾ وَمَا عَلَيۡنَآ إِلَّا ٱلۡبَلَٰغُ ٱلۡمُبِينُ ﴿١٧﴾ قَالُوٓاْ
إِنَّا تَطَيَّرۡنَا بِكُمۡۖ لَئِن لَّمۡ تَنتَهُواْ لَنَرۡجُمَنَّكُمۡ وَلَيَمَسَّنَّكُم مِّنَّا
عَذَابٌ أَلِيمٞ ﴿١٨﴾ قَالُواْ طَٰٓئِرُكُم مَّعَكُمۡۚ أَئِن ذُكِّرۡتُمۚ بَلۡ
أَنتُمۡ قَوۡمٞ مُّسۡرِفُونَ ﴿١٩﴾ وَجَآءَ مِنۡ أَقۡصَا ٱلۡمَدِينَةِ
رَجُلٞ يَسۡعَىٰ قَالَ يَٰقَوۡمِ ٱتَّبِعُواْ ٱلۡمُرۡسَلِينَ ﴿٢٠﴾ ٱتَّبِعُواْ
مَن لَّا يَسۡـَٔلُكُمۡ أَجۡرٗا وَهُم مُّهۡتَدُونَ ﴿٢١﴾ وَمَا لِيَ لَآ أَعۡبُدُ
ٱلَّذِي فَطَرَنِي وَإِلَيۡهِ تُرۡجَعُونَ ﴿٢٢﴾ ءَأَتَّخِذُ مِن دُونِهِۦٓ
ءَالِهَةً إِن يُرِدۡنِ ٱلرَّحۡمَٰنُ بِضُرّٖ لَّا تُغۡنِ عَنِّي شَفَٰعَتُهُمۡ شَيۡـٔٗا
وَلَا يُنقِذُونِ ﴿٢٣﴾ إِنِّيٓ إِذٗا لَّفِي ضَلَٰلٖ مُّبِينٍ ﴿٢٤﴾ إِنِّيٓ
ءَامَنتُ بِرَبِّكُمۡ فَٱسۡمَعُونِ ﴿٢٥﴾ قِيلَ ٱدۡخُلِ ٱلۡجَنَّةَۖ قَالَ
يَٰلَيۡتَ قَوۡمِي يَعۡلَمُونَ ﴿٢٦﴾ بِمَا غَفَرَ لِي رَبِّي وَجَعَلَنِي مِنَ
ٱلۡمُكۡرَمِينَ ﴿٢٧﴾ ۞ وَمَآ أَنزَلۡنَا عَلَىٰ قَوۡمِهِۦ مِنۢ بَعۡدِهِۦ مِن
جُندٖ مِّنَ ٱلسَّمَآءِ وَمَا كُنَّا مُنزِلِينَ ﴿٢٨﴾ إِن كَانَتۡ إِلَّا
صَيۡحَةٗ وَٰحِدَةٗ فَإِذَا هُمۡ خَٰمِدُونَ ﴿٢٩﴾ يَٰحَسۡرَةً عَلَى
ٱلۡعِبَادِۚ مَا يَأۡتِيهِم مِّن رَّسُولٍ إِلَّا كَانُواْ بِهِۦ يَسۡتَهۡزِءُونَ ﴿٣٠﴾

أَلَمْ يَرَوْاْ كَمْ أَهْلَكْنَا قَبْلَهُم مِّنَ ٱلْقُرُونِ أَنَّهُمْ إِلَيْهِمْ لَا
يَرْجِعُونَ ﴿٣١﴾ وَإِن كُلٌّ لَّمَّا جَمِيعٌ لَّدَيْنَا مُحْضَرُونَ ﴿٣٢﴾
وَءَايَةٌ لَّهُمُ ٱلْأَرْضُ ٱلْمَيْتَةُ أَحْيَيْنَٰهَا وَأَخْرَجْنَا مِنْهَا حَبًّا
فَمِنْهُ يَأْكُلُونَ ﴿٣٣﴾ وَجَعَلْنَا فِيهَا جَنَّٰتٍ مِّن نَّخِيلٍ
وَأَعْنَٰبٍ وَفَجَّرْنَا فِيهَا مِنَ ٱلْعُيُونِ ﴿٣٤﴾ لِيَأْكُلُواْ مِن
ثَمَرِهِۦ وَمَا عَمِلَتْهُ أَيْدِيهِمْ ۖ أَفَلَا يَشْكُرُونَ ﴿٣٥﴾ سُبْحَٰنَ
ٱلَّذِى خَلَقَ ٱلْأَزْوَٰجَ كُلَّهَا مِمَّا تُنۢبِتُ ٱلْأَرْضُ وَمِنْ
أَنفُسِهِمْ وَمِمَّا لَا يَعْلَمُونَ ﴿٣٦﴾ وَءَايَةٌ لَّهُمُ ٱلَّيْلُ نَسْلَخُ
مِنْهُ ٱلنَّهَارَ فَإِذَا هُم مُّظْلِمُونَ ﴿٣٧﴾ وَٱلشَّمْسُ تَجْرِى
لِمُسْتَقَرٍّ لَّهَا ۚ ذَٰلِكَ تَقْدِيرُ ٱلْعَزِيزِ ٱلْعَلِيمِ ﴿٣٨﴾ وَٱلْقَمَرَ
قَدَّرْنَٰهُ مَنَازِلَ حَتَّىٰ عَادَ كَٱلْعُرْجُونِ ٱلْقَدِيمِ ﴿٣٩﴾ لَا
ٱلشَّمْسُ يَنۢبَغِى لَهَآ أَن تُدْرِكَ ٱلْقَمَرَ وَلَا ٱلَّيْلُ سَابِقُ
ٱلنَّهَارِ ۚ وَكُلٌّ فِى فَلَكٍ يَسْبَحُونَ ﴿٤٠﴾ وَءَايَةٌ لَّهُمْ أَنَّا حَمَلْنَا
ذُرِّيَّتَهُمْ فِى ٱلْفُلْكِ ٱلْمَشْحُونِ ﴿٤١﴾ وَخَلَقْنَا لَهُم مِّن مِّثْلِهِۦ
مَا يَرْكَبُونَ ﴿٤٢﴾ وَإِن نَّشَأْ نُغْرِقْهُمْ فَلَا صَرِيخَ لَهُمْ وَلَا هُمْ
يُنقَذُونَ ﴿٤٣﴾ إِلَّا رَحْمَةً مِّنَّا وَمَتَٰعًا إِلَىٰ حِينٍ ﴿٤٤﴾ وَإِذَا قِيلَ
لَهُمُ ٱتَّقُواْ مَا بَيْنَ أَيْدِيكُمْ وَمَا خَلْفَكُمْ لَعَلَّكُمْ تُرْحَمُونَ ﴿٤٥﴾

وَمَا تَأۡتِيهِم مِّنۡ ءَايَةٖ مِّنۡ ءَايَٰتِ رَبِّهِمۡ إِلَّا كَانُواْ عَنۡهَا
مُعۡرِضِينَ ٤٦ وَإِذَا قِيلَ لَهُمۡ أَنفِقُواْ مِمَّا رَزَقَكُمُ ٱللَّهُ قَالَ
ٱلَّذِينَ كَفَرُواْ لِلَّذِينَ ءَامَنُوٓاْ أَنُطۡعِمُ مَن لَّوۡ يَشَآءُ ٱللَّهُ
أَطۡعَمَهُۥٓ إِنۡ أَنتُمۡ إِلَّا فِي ضَلَٰلٖ مُّبِينٖ ٤٧ وَيَقُولُونَ مَتَىٰ
هَٰذَا ٱلۡوَعۡدُ إِن كُنتُمۡ صَٰدِقِينَ ٤٨ مَا يَنظُرُونَ إِلَّا
صَيۡحَةٗ وَٰحِدَةٗ تَأۡخُذُهُمۡ وَهُمۡ يَخِصِّمُونَ ٤٩ فَلَا
يَسۡتَطِيعُونَ تَوۡصِيَةٗ وَلَآ إِلَىٰٓ أَهۡلِهِمۡ يَرۡجِعُونَ ٥٠ وَنُفِخَ
فِي ٱلصُّورِ فَإِذَا هُم مِّنَ ٱلۡأَجۡدَاثِ إِلَىٰ رَبِّهِمۡ يَنسِلُونَ
٥١ قَالُواْ يَٰوَيۡلَنَا مَنۢ بَعَثَنَا مِن مَّرۡقَدِنَاۜۗ هَٰذَا مَا وَعَدَ
ٱلرَّحۡمَٰنُ وَصَدَقَ ٱلۡمُرۡسَلُونَ ٥٢ إِن كَانَتۡ إِلَّا
صَيۡحَةٗ وَٰحِدَةٗ فَإِذَا هُمۡ جَمِيعٞ لَّدَيۡنَا مُحۡضَرُونَ ٥٣ فَٱلۡيَوۡمَ
لَا تُظۡلَمُ نَفۡسٞ شَيۡـٔٗا وَلَا تُجۡزَوۡنَ إِلَّا مَا كُنتُمۡ تَعۡمَلُونَ
٥٤ إِنَّ أَصۡحَٰبَ ٱلۡجَنَّةِ ٱلۡيَوۡمَ فِي شُغُلٖ فَٰكِهُونَ ٥٥ هُمۡ
وَأَزۡوَٰجُهُمۡ فِي ظِلَٰلٍ عَلَى ٱلۡأَرَآئِكِ مُتَّكِـُٔونَ ٥٦ لَهُمۡ فِيهَا
فَٰكِهَةٞ وَلَهُم مَّا يَدَّعُونَ ٥٧ سَلَٰمٞ قَوۡلٗا مِّن رَّبّٖ رَّحِيمٖ
٥٨ وَٱمۡتَٰزُواْ ٱلۡيَوۡمَ أَيُّهَا ٱلۡمُجۡرِمُونَ ٥٩ ۞ أَلَمۡ أَعۡهَدۡ
إِلَيۡكُمۡ يَٰبَنِيٓ ءَادَمَ أَن لَّا تَعۡبُدُواْ ٱلشَّيۡطَٰنَۖ إِنَّهُۥ لَكُمۡ
عَدُوّٞ مُّبِينٞ ٦٠ وَأَنِ ٱعۡبُدُونِيۚ هَٰذَا صِرَٰطٞ مُّسۡتَقِيمٞ ٦١

وَلَقَدْ أَضَلَّ مِنكُمْ جِبِلًّا كَثِيرًا ۖ أَفَلَمْ تَكُونُوا۟ تَعْقِلُونَ
﴿٦٢﴾ هَٰذِهِۦ جَهَنَّمُ ٱلَّتِى كُنتُمْ تُوعَدُونَ ﴿٦٣﴾
ٱصْلَوْهَا ٱلْيَوْمَ بِمَا كُنتُمْ تَكْفُرُونَ ﴿٦٤﴾ ٱلْيَوْمَ نَخْتِمُ
عَلَىٰٓ أَفْوَٰهِهِمْ وَتُكَلِّمُنَآ أَيْدِيهِمْ وَتَشْهَدُ أَرْجُلُهُم بِمَا
كَانُوا۟ يَكْسِبُونَ ﴿٦٥﴾ وَلَوْ نَشَآءُ لَطَمَسْنَا عَلَىٰٓ أَعْيُنِهِمْ
فَٱسْتَبَقُوا۟ ٱلصِّرَٰطَ فَأَنَّىٰ يُبْصِرُونَ ﴿٦٦﴾ وَلَوْ نَشَآءُ
لَمَسَخْنَٰهُمْ عَلَىٰ مَكَانَتِهِمْ فَمَا ٱسْتَطَٰعُوا۟ مُضِيًّا وَلَا
يَرْجِعُونَ ﴿٦٧﴾ وَمَن نُّعَمِّرْهُ نُنَكِّسْهُ فِى ٱلْخَلْقِ ۖ أَفَلَا
يَعْقِلُونَ ﴿٦٨﴾ وَمَا عَلَّمْنَٰهُ ٱلشِّعْرَ وَمَا يَنۢبَغِى لَهُۥٓ ۚ إِنْ هُوَ
إِلَّا ذِكْرٌ وَقُرْءَانٌ مُّبِينٌ ﴿٦٩﴾ لِّيُنذِرَ مَن كَانَ حَيًّا وَيَحِقَّ
ٱلْقَوْلُ عَلَى ٱلْكَٰفِرِينَ ﴿٧٠﴾ أَوَلَمْ يَرَوْا۟ أَنَّا خَلَقْنَا لَهُم
مِّمَّا عَمِلَتْ أَيْدِينَآ أَنْعَٰمًا فَهُمْ لَهَا مَٰلِكُونَ ﴿٧١﴾
وَذَلَّلْنَٰهَا لَهُمْ فَمِنْهَا رَكُوبُهُمْ وَمِنْهَا يَأْكُلُونَ ﴿٧٢﴾ وَلَهُمْ
فِيهَا مَنَٰفِعُ وَمَشَارِبُ ۖ أَفَلَا يَشْكُرُونَ ﴿٧٣﴾ وَٱتَّخَذُوا۟ مِن
دُونِ ٱللَّهِ ءَالِهَةً لَّعَلَّهُمْ يُنصَرُونَ ﴿٧٤﴾ لَا يَسْتَطِيعُونَ
نَصْرَهُمْ وَهُمْ لَهُمْ جُندٌ مُّحْضَرُونَ ﴿٧٥﴾ فَلَا يَحْزُنكَ
قَوْلُهُمْ ۘ إِنَّا نَعْلَمُ مَا يُسِرُّونَ وَمَا يُعْلِنُونَ ﴿٧٦﴾ أَوَلَمْ يَرَ
ٱلْإِنسَٰنُ أَنَّا خَلَقْنَٰهُ مِن نُّطْفَةٍ فَإِذَا هُوَ خَصِيمٌ مُّبِينٌ ﴿٧٧﴾

وَضَرَبَ لَنَا مَثَلًا وَنَسِيَ خَلْقَهُۥ ۖ قَالَ مَن يُحْيِ ٱلْعِظَٰمَ
وَهِيَ رَمِيمٌ ﴿٧٨﴾ قُلْ يُحْيِيهَا ٱلَّذِيٓ أَنشَأَهَآ أَوَّلَ مَرَّةٍ ۖ وَهُوَ
بِكُلِّ خَلْقٍ عَلِيمٌ ﴿٧٩﴾ ٱلَّذِي جَعَلَ لَكُم مِّنَ ٱلشَّجَرِ
ٱلْأَخْضَرِ نَارًا فَإِذَآ أَنتُم مِّنْهُ تُوقِدُونَ ﴿٨٠﴾ أَوَلَيْسَ ٱلَّذِي
خَلَقَ ٱلسَّمَٰوَٰتِ وَٱلْأَرْضَ بِقَٰدِرٍ عَلَىٰٓ أَن يَخْلُقَ مِثْلَهُم ۚ بَلَىٰ
وَهُوَ ٱلْخَلَّٰقُ ٱلْعَلِيمُ ﴿٨١﴾ إِنَّمَآ أَمْرُهُۥٓ إِذَآ أَرَادَ شَيْـًٔا أَن
يَقُولَ لَهُۥ كُن فَيَكُونُ ﴿٨٢﴾ فَسُبْحَٰنَ ٱلَّذِي بِيَدِهِۦ
مَلَكُوتُ كُلِّ شَيْءٍ وَإِلَيْهِ تُرْجَعُونَ ﴿٨٣﴾

يس والقرآن الحكيم